George Frederick Root

First Years in Song-Land

George Frederick Root

First Years in Song-Land

ISBN/EAN: 9783337376208

Printed in Europe, USA, Canada, Australia, Japan

Cover: Foto ©Thomas Meinert / pixelio.de

More available books at **www.hansebooks.com**

FIRST YEARS

IN

SONG-LAND

A SINGING BOOK

FOR

Day Schools and Juvenile Singing Classes,

CONTAINING

CAREFULLY GRADED LESSONS & MUSICAL EXERCISES,

WITH

Songs for Imitation Practice; Songs for the Study
of Notation; Songs for Recreation; and Songs
and Hymns for Special Occasions.

BY

GEO. F. ROOT.

CINCINNATI:

Published by The JOHN CHURCH CO. 74 W. Fourth St.

CHICAGO:
Root & Sons Music Co.
200 Wabash Ave.

NEW YORK:
J. Church & Co.
55 East 13th St.

PREFACE.

At what age should children commence learning to read music?

As the child learns to talk before it learns letters, so it should learn to sing before it learns notes. As the child learns its first words and phrases by imitation, so it should learn its first songs.

When the child can read, and has commenced other school studies, it may commence the study of Notation, but it should keep on singing while it is acquiring the ability to read music.

This book is full of songs that may be used for imitation singing, the importance of which can hardly be over-estimated.

If it is asked, Why is this so important?—the answer is: Music is essentially an imitative art, and at any stage of progress its best results are obtained according to this law. As to children, they are absolutely molded in their pronunciation, quality of tone, and style of performance, by the examples they hear. The musical foundation, good or bad, is laid at this time of conscious or unconscious imitation.

And beside this, all matters of voice culture, proper breathing, purity of tone, good expression, distinct utterance, etc., can be better taught and learned while the children's minds are free from thoughts of Notation. In fact, children should bring to the study of Notation, good habits already formed in these things.

A book can not be a teacher, nor a substitute for one, but it can have ideas about teaching, and can state the facts from which teaching is done, or, perhaps more truly, it can state the facts that teaching develops. But the great desideratum, in a musical collection for school work, is a well-ordered, interesting, and carefully-graded course of elementary lessons, and a generous supply of good, attractive songs and hymns for the singing hour, and for the many occasions that arise during the school year, when singing is wanted.

It is confidently believed that in all these respects the present work is far in advance of any of its predecessors.

G. F. R.

Notation and Practice Lessons.

———:✳:———

CHAPTER I.

TONE-PROPERTIES AND THEIR DEPARTMENTS.

(Introducing and teaching these subjects is left to the teacher. These statements are for record and reference *after* the work has been done. The teacher may do more or less of this theoretical work according to the age of the pupils, but the lessons for practice should be taken in order.)

1. A musical sound is called a *Tone*.
2. In every tone there is a *Length*, a *Pitch*, a *Power*, and a *Quality*.
3. The *duration* of a tone is called its length.
4. The *highness* or *lowness* of a tone is called its pitch.
5. The *loudness* or *softness* of a tone is called its power.
6. The *character* of a tone is called its quality.

NOTE.—We tell one voice from another by its quality. The difference between a flute tone and a violin tone is a difference of quality. The same voice can make a joyful tone and a sad tone, a clear tone and a somber tone; and these are differences—not of length, pitch or power, but of quality. There are good qualities and bad qualities, but some kind of quality every tone must have.

7. The study of music really consists in the study of the lengths, pitches, powers, and qualities of tones.
8. These are called *tone-lengths*, *tone-pitches*, *tone-powers* and *tone-qualities*, and are known as the *properties* of tones.

NOTE.—"Departments" may not be necessary here, but as a knowledge of them is convenient, and as their introduction is but a matter of a few minutes, the class would not be long delayed by bringing them in now.

9. As in mathematics the different ways of treating numbers are shown in the terms Addition, Subtraction, Multiplication, etc., so in music the different ways of regarding tones are shown and included in the terms *Rhythmics*, *Melodics* and *Dynamics*, which are said to be departments in music.
10. Tone lengths, with their names and representations, and every thing they cause, belong to Rhythmics.
11. Tone-pitches and all things that belong to them are in Melodics.
12. Tone-powers and tone-qualities, with all their names and representations, are in Dynamics.

NOTE.—The writer has found it both profitable and interesting to a class to place the names of these departments (Rhythmics, Melodics and Dynamics) at the top of a spare blackboard or large sheet of dark paper (something that need not be disturbed), and as fast as new topics are introduced let the class say under which head they shall be placed, and so get an orderly record of every sign, name and term used in the course.

13. When people speak intelligently of the *rhythmic* character of a piece of music, they mean something about the tone-lengths used, or their accents, or the measure or movement in which they go—(for these latter things are caused by lengths.)
14. When people speak of the *melodic* character of music, they mean something about the pitches used, their pleasant or peculiar succession, their heighth or their depth. It is variation of pitches that makes melody.
15. When people speak of the *dynamic* character of music, they mean something about the loudness of the tones (tone-powers), or the sweetness, or sadness, or joyfulness of the tones (tone-qualities), or of both combined, as loud and joyful, soft and sad, etc.

NOTE.—The author's questions will be found all together at the end of the course, in case the teacher would like to see or make use of them.

CHAPTER II.

NOTES, BEATS AND MEASURES.

16. Although every tone must have length, pitch, power and quality, we may attend to one of these things at a time. Let us begin with tone-lengths.

17. Sing eight tones with "la" about as fast as the pulse beats—(any convenient pitch, but keep the same pitch throughout.)

18. These lengths are called *Quarters*.

19. These quarters are represented to the eye by *Quarter Notes*, thus:

La, la, la, la, la, la, la, la, la, la, la, la, la, la, la, la.

Sing this lesson *by note*.

20. Sing four tones, each as long as two quarters.

21. These lengths are called *Halves*.

22. These lengths are represented by characters called *Half Notes*:

La, la, la, la, la, la, la, la.

23. Sing these lengths again and *think* of two quarters while you sing each half.

24. Sing alternately two quarters and one half, two quarters and one half, until all can do it.

La, la, la, la, la, la, la, la, la, la, la, la.

25. Sing it again, and notice that the *thought* of quarters while singing is like pulsations in the mind, one pulsation with each quarter, and two with each half.

26. These pulsations are called *Beats*.

27. These beats group themselves into twos, as they go in this lesson. Groups of beats are called *Measures*.

28. When the measures consist of two beats each they are called *Double Measures*.

29. A downward motion of the hand goes with the first beat in the measure, and an upward motion of the hand with the second beat in the measure. This is called *Beating Time*.

NOTE.—Where the children are small they ought to be kept quite a long time on each of these points. For example, " beating time " in these double measures, and singing three or four of these lessons, might occupy them a week.

30. Measures are represented to the eye by spaces between upright lines called *Bars*, thus:

La, la, la, la, la, la, la, la, la, la, la, la.

Notes are put into the written measures here to show the lengths that are wanted.

31. The bar at the end is called a *Double Bar* or *Close*.

Sing and beat the following lessons:

La, la, la, la, la, la, la, la, la, la, la, la, la, la.
Tones of song in meas-ures flow, Sometimes fast and sometimes slow;

La, la, la, la, la, la, la, la, la, la, la, la, la.
Fast and slow, fast and slow, Sometimes fast and sometimes slow.

CHAPTER III.

PITCH, STAFF AND CLEFS.

32. Sing eight quarters, syllable "do," at this pitch. (Teacher gives C.)

33. You sang but one pitch then, though you sang it several times. The name of this pitch is *C.*

34. Let us make a notation for this pitch just to use for a moment:

C,	C,	C,	C,	C,	C,	C,	C.
Do,	do,	do,	do,	do,	do,	do,	do.

35. Sing this pitch, named C, from the above notation, without beating time or trying to make measures.

36. Let us get a little nearer to the regular musical notation. Let the *short line* below the *five long ones* stand for this pitch, C. Sing the lesson from this notation:

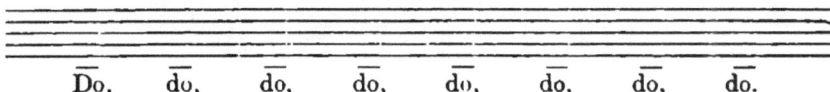

Do, do, do, do, do, do, do, do.

37. Sing eight quarters, syllable "re," at this pitch. (Teacher gives D.)

38. Sing this lesson from our temporary notation, without beating time, making quarter lengths:

D,	D,	D,	D,	D,	D,	D,	D.
Re,	re,	re,	re,	re,	re,	re,	re.

39. Sing this lesson in the same way:

C,	C,	C,	C,	D,	D,	D,	D,	C,	D,	C,	D,	C,	D,	C.
Do,	do,	do,	do,	re,	re,	re,	re,	do,	re,	do,	re,	do,	re,	do.

40. The space between the short line and the first long one often stands for this pitch, D. It will be easier to see whether the line or the space is wanted if notes are used—a note upon the short line when C is to be sung, and a note upon the space when D is to be sung.

41. As you are singing *quarter lengths,* we will use *quarter notes.*

Sing from this notation:

Do, do, do, do, re, re, re, re, do, re, do, re, do, re, do.

42. The different pitches of tones are represented by lines and by the spaces between them, and by the *spaces above* and *below* them. Combined these lines and spaces form what is called the *Staff.*

43. The staff always has five long lines, but is often enlarged by short lines above or below. The names of the lines in this staff are,—line below, 1st line, 2d line, 3d line, 4th line and 5th line. The names of the spaces here are 2d space below, space below, 1st space, 2d space, 3d space, 4th space, and space above. Every staff begins and ends with a space.

44. Each line or space of the staff is called a *Degree.*

45. Sometimes the staff is so arranged that the second space stands for C. The staff is so arranged by placing a character called the *Base Clef* upon it.

46. When the staff is so arranged that the line below stands for C, a character called a *Treble Clef* is placed upon it.

47. We can now combine lengths and pitches. Notes, measures and staff, and so attend to both Rhythmics and Melodics at the same time.

48. The figure 2 stands for double measure. The figure 4 stands for quarter note. The two figures form the *Measure Sign*, and say "two quarters or their value in each measure." The length that exactly coincides with the beat is called the *Beat-note*. The quarter note is here the beat-note.

49. Now sing and "beat time."

Do, do, do,   do, do, do,   do, do, do, do, do, do, do.
{ Quar-ter, half, quar-ter, half, Line be - low and treb - le staff;
{ Quar-ter, half, quar-ter, half, Pitch of C and treb - le staff.

50. Practice again the pitches C and D.

Do, do, do, do, re, re, re,   do, do, re, re, do, re, do.
{ Now be-gin, be - gin with care, Tho'ts right here and not else-where;
{ Let no one his neigh-bor view, Till we've sung the les - son through.

51. Practice the new pitch, E, syllable "mi."

52. Sing this lesson in our temporary notation.   Make quarter lengths.

C, C, C, C, D, D, D, D, E, E, E, E, D, D, D, D, Ċ.
Do, do, do, do, re, re, re, re, mi, mi, mi, mi, re, re, re, re, do.

53. Now sing the same pitches in the usual notation, but in a different order, and making a different tune.   Now beat time and make measures.

Do, do, re, re, mi, mi, re,   do, do, re, re, mi, re, do.
{ Let no voic-es   si - lent be, But let all sing full and free ;
{ Each attend to "num-ber one," That his work may be well done.

Practice the following lessons with syllables only.   When they are well learned, try singing them softly.   Do not fail to "beat time."

54.

55.

56.

57.

58. Practice the new pitch, F, with syllable "fa."

59. Sing the following preparatory lesson. In these preparatory lessons there need be no attempt at making measures.

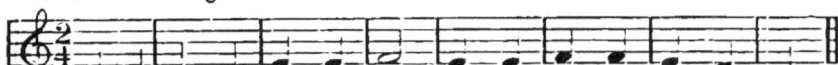

C,   D,   E,   E,   F,   F,   E,   E,   F,   F,   E,   E,   D,   D,   C

Do,   re,   mi,   mi,   fa,   fa,   mi,   mi,   fa,   fa,   mi,   mi,   re,   re,   do

60. Now in the regular notation. Notice the hints in the words.

Do, do, re,   re,   mi, mi,   fa,   mi,   mi,   fa,   fa,   mi,   re,   do.

{ Of po - si - tion take great care, Form e - rect and shoulders square;

{ All good habits now be - gin, If the song-prize you would win.

Syllables only. Learn thoroughly. Speak, or rather sing, the syllables distinctly. Form the habit of "beating time." It might be well to name the pitches of each lesson before singing.

61.

62.

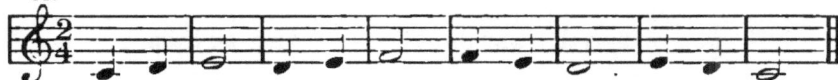

63.

64.

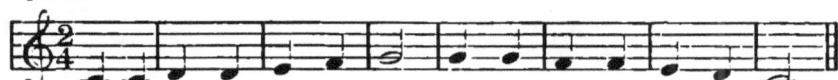

65. Practice the new pitch, G, with the syllable "sol."

66. Sing the following preparatory lesson:

C,   D,   E,   F,   G,   G,   G,   G,   G,   F,   E,   D,   C,   C,   C,   C.

Do,   re,   mi,   fa,   sol,   sol,   sol,   sol,   sol,   fa,   mi,   re,   do,   do,   do,   do.

67. The new pitch represented in the regular way.

The writer would question about the pitches represented, and the degrees of the staff that represent them.

Do, do, re,   re,   mi,   fa,   sol,   sol,   sol,   fa,   fa,   mi,   re,   do.

{ Let the breath be deep and full, Quick and noiseless, that's the rule:

{ Does it last throughout the line, While we sing and beat the time?

Name pitches and degrees of staff that represent them. After learning each lesson thoroughly with syllables, sing it first with a tone of medium strength, then softly.

68.

69.

70.

71.

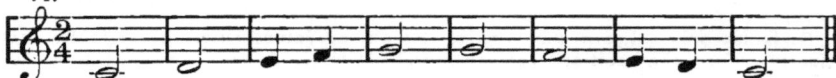

72. Practice the new pitch, A, with syllable "la."
73. Sing the following preparatory lesson:

C,　D,　E,　F,　G,　G,　A,　A,　A,　G,　F,　E,　D,　D,　C,　C.
Do, re, mi, fa, sol, sol, la, la, la, sol, fa, mi, re, re, do, do.

74. Now the new pitch regularly represented.

Do, re, mi, mi, fa, sol, la, la, la, sol, fa, mi, re, do.
Rules like these, as we shall find, We must keep in sight and mind,
Till we know them thro' and thro', Ev-'ry thing we have to do.

What pitches? What degrees of staff used? What lengths? What syllables? Vary strength of voice. Speak distinctly.

75.

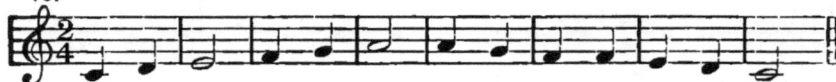

76.

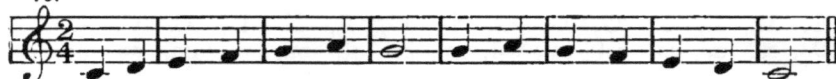

77.

78.

79. Practice the new pitch, B, with syllable "si;" also the C next above it, syllable "do."

80. One more preparatory exercise, "quarter" lengths.

C, D, E, F, G, G, G, G, A, A, A, A, B, B, B, B, C.
Do, re, mi, fa, sol, sol, sol, sol, la, la, la, la, si, si, si, si, do.

81. Regular notation. Observe that the upper C makes a good ending as well as the lower C. This is the basis of an important principle that we shall understand by and by.

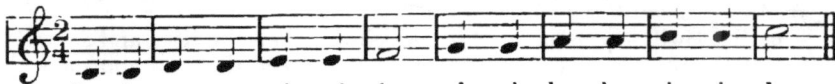

Do, do, re, re, mi, mi, fa, sol, sol, la, la, si, si, do.
{ Do we still approach the prize, As our voic-es up-ward rise?
{ Are we right or are we wrong In po-si-tion, breath and song?

Be careful that the high pitches are sweet and pure. That is more difficult to acquire than loudness of tone. Can you now give the syllables readily?

82.

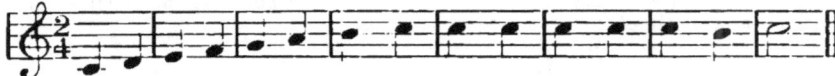

83.

84.

85.

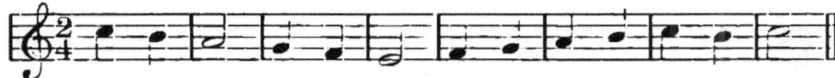

Good Morning!

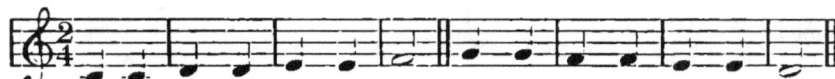

1. Now, good morning, one and all! Hear ye not our mu-sic's call?
2. Now the bird for-sakes his nest; See his proud-ly swell-ing breast,
3. So we sing our morning song; We have sung it oft and long;

Wake from slumbers, greet the sun, For his long night's work is done.
While he gai - ly soars on high, Sing-ing sweet-ly thro' the sky.
Ev - 'ry morn 'tis fresh and new, As the pearl-y drops of dew.

Down the Hill.

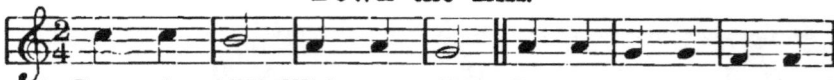

1. Down the hill! With a will! Do not fear the win-ter's
2. Clear the way! No de-lay! Win-ter will not al-ways
3. Down the hill! With a will! Nev-er mind a lit-tle

chill; Swift-ly go, All a-glow, O'er the ice and snow.
stay; In a row Now we go O'er the ice and snow.
spill; In a row Off we go, O'er the ice and snow.

CHAPTER IV.

TONE-POWERS AND TONE-QUALITIES.

86. Now let us attend to Tone-powers.

Teach *mezzo, forte, piano* and *pianissimo*, and their abbreviations; then give the class a convenient pitch and let them sing the following lessons. Let the lengths be quarters (about as fast as pulse-beats.) Sing each power to the syllable "la," without beating time.

m   m   m   m   p   p   p   p   m   m   m   m   f   f   f   f
La, la, la, la, la, la, la, la, la, la, la, la, la, la, la, la.

87.

f   f   f   f   m   m   m   m   p   p   p   p   pp   pp   pp   pp
La, la, la, la, la, la, la, la, la, la, la, la, la, la, la, la.

NOTE.—There is a power called *fortissimo* (*ff*), meaning very loud, but it should be almost never used in children's singing.

88. Now let us combine Tone-lengths, Tone-pitches, Tone-powers and Measures by means of the proper representations. The effect of a power sign continues until it is contradicted by another. There are soft powers as well as loud powers. Use syllables.

89.

90.

91. Sing syllables first. Observe that the words would indicate the different powers that are marked.

Me-dium is the breez-es power, Stronger when the storm-clouds low'r,

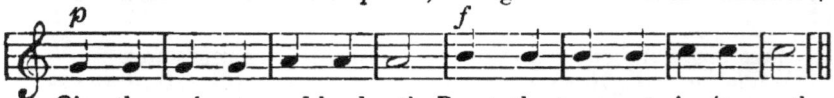

O'er the qui-et wood-land path, Bursts the tem-pest in its wrath.

92. Now let us attend to Tone-qualities.

Somber tones are made by distending the back part of the mouth (the opening into the throat), and clear tones are made by avoiding such distension. If thought best, these tone-qualities can be practiced before the following lesson is sung.

93. The following lesson combines Tone-lengths, Tone-pitches, Tone-powers and Tone-qualities, and the measures in which all Tone-properties must flow in order to make music. Sing the lesson with syllables first. Do not omit beating time.

Dark the night! Dark the night! But with morning comes the light;

Bright the day! Bright the day! Till the daylight fades a-way.

94. In the foregoing lesson all the tone-properties are represented—the lengths by notes (the notes also point out which lines and spaces are wanted); the pitches by lines and spaces; the powers by *m, f, p,* etc., and the qualities by clear, somber, joyfully, etc. It is customary, however, to use Italian terms to indicate quality; as *giojoso,* for "joyfully;" but these will come in due time. It is only important to say here, that while lengths and pitches must always be represented, powers and qualities may often be left to the discretion of the performer, or are plainly enough indicated by the sense and sentiment of the words that are sung. In written music you always see notes and lines and spaces (length and pitch signs), but very often the power and quality signs are omitted, for the reasons given above.

Joyful Sing.

The words here are a sure guide to the quality of tone and the powers that should here be used. Sing syllables first.

1. Joy - ful sing, the sum-mer's com - ing, Hap-py voic-es, hap-py hearts;
2. Hark! the wild birds' songs are ring-ing; Hap-py voic-es, hap-py hearts;

Old and young, with glad-ness beam-ing, Come, oh! come, and take your parts.
Old and young, come join the sing-ing, Quick-ly come and take your parts.

The Song of the Autumn Leaves.

These words show very plainly the power and quality to be used. No need of marking them.

1. We are fad-ing, we are fall - ing; Chil-dren, list - en while you may;
2. We are fad-ing, we are fall - ing From the branch-es brown and sere;

We are call - ing, we are call - ing, Thro' the dim au - tum-nal day.
Children, we to you are call - ing; To our fare - well song give ear.

CHAPTER V.

RELATIVE PITCH NAMES, BASE CLEF.

95. The names of pitches that we have used thus far are called *Absolute Names.* We should now become familiar with what are called the *Relative Names* of pitches. These are the same as the names of numbers, and for the present are applied as follows: one to C, two to D, three to E, four to F, five to G, six to A, seven to B, and eight to the upper C.

NOTE TO THE TEACHER.—The writer would not give the *reasons* for absolute and relative pitch names now. He would for the present ask the class to take his word for their necessity. When other keys are introduced, both the reasons and necessity for the two kinds of naming wil' easily be made to appear.

96. Will the teacher call for pitches by their relative names, the pupils applying syllables, before singing the following notation of the same?

1 1 | 2 2 | 3 3 | 4 4 | 5 5 | 6 6 | 7 7 | 8 8 {
Do, do, re, re, mi, mi, fa, fa, sol, sol, la, la, si, si, do, do,
Now from names of num-bers sing-ing, Clear-ly let each voice be ring-ing;

8 8 | 7 7 | 6 6 | 5 5 | 4 4 | 3 3 | 2 2 | 1 1 ||
do, do, si, si, la, la, sol, sol, fa, fa, mi, mi, re, re, do, do.
Firm-ly, too, while we're de - scend-ing, Keep the voic - es   to   the   end-ing.

97. Will the teacher now introduce and practice skips, by calling for the tones by their numerical names? Especially let the class be able to sing 1, 3, 5 and 8 in any order.

Practice the following lessons carefully with syllables. In exercises of this kind no thought need be given to power and quality. About *mezzo* would naturally be used. Give the numeral or relative names of the tones to be sung.

98.

99.

100.

101.

102.
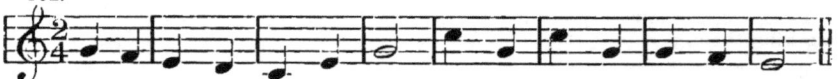

103.

104.

105. Sing this lesson first with syllables, then words. Give the power and quality that the words call for. Then divide the class into four sections and sing the piece as a round. Let the second division commence when the first has sung four measures, let the third division commence when the second has sung four measures, etc.

See the har-bor from the shore! Like a glass-y mirrored floor;

Hear the dis-tant breakers roar! See the o - cean wide, be - fore!

106. When this lesson is learned, it may be sung as a round for four divisions, or there may be as many divisions as measures. It may be sung by seats or sections. While the divisions are singing "round and round," the teacher might call "mezzo," "piano," "forte," etc., to vary the powers.

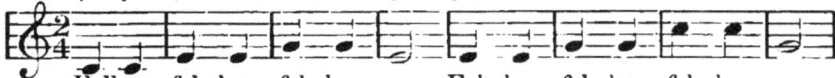

Follow, fol - low, fol - low me, Fol - low, fol - low, fol - low me,

And the for - est lights and shadows You shall sure-ly, surely see.

Don't Take Offense.

Syllables first. Power and quality indicated by words. It is well to give absolute and relative names of pitches to be sung.

1. Be not swift to take of - fense, An - ger is a foe to sense;
2. Ech-o not an an - gry word, Think how oft - en you have erred;

Brood not dark-ly o'er a wrong, Which will dis - ap-pear ere long.
Time its ran-cor will a - bate; Do not, then, re-sent, but wait.

Come, Let's Sing.

It is not difficult to see what powers and qualities should be used here. Notice that there is something in this song that inclines you to sing faster than you have been singing.

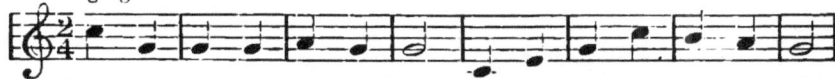

1. Come, let's sing a mer-ry round; Wake the cheerful, cheerful glee;
2. En - vy, an - ger, hence, a - way! E - vil tho'ts and pas-sions flee;

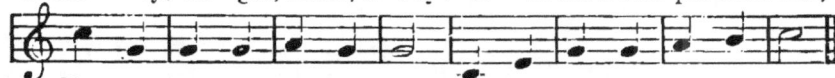

Sing a - loud with joy - ful sound, Hap - py, hap - py songsters we.
Why should we indulge them? say, Why should you, or why should we?

The April Shower.

Power and quality plainly indicated by words.   Syllables first.   Do not forget to
"beat time."

1. Pat-ter, pat-ter, let   it   pour; Pat-ter, pat-ter, let   it   roar;
2. Pat-ter, pat-ter, let   it   pour; Pat-ter, pat-ter, let   it   roar;
3. Pat-ter, pat-ter, let   it   pour; Pat-ter, pat-ter, let   it   roar;

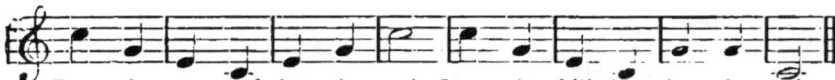

Down the steep roof let   it   rush, Down the hill-side   let   it   gush.
Let   the gau-dy light-ning flash, Let   the head-long thun-der dash.
Soon the clouds will burst a - way, Soon will shine the bright spring day.

107. The Base Clef makes the staff represent pitches in a new way. The lines
and spaces are the same and have the same names as before (space below, first line,
first space, etc.,) but now "second space" stands for C, "third line" for D, etc.

Do, do, re, re, mi, mi, fa, fa, sol, sol, la, la, si, si, do,
Let us now be up and do-ing, With a heart for a - ny fate;

do, do, si, si, la, la, sol, sol, fa, fa, mi, mi, re, re, do.
Still achieving, still pur - su - ing, Learn to   la - bor and to wait.

108. Let every one learn to sing as readily from the Base Clef as from the
Treble Clef.   Sing absolute and relative names of pitches to be sung.

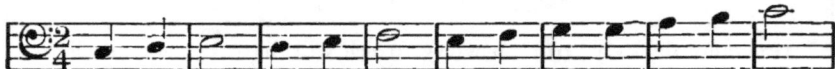

Do, re, mi, re, mi, fa, mi, fa, sol, sol, la, si, do,

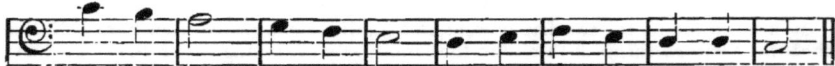

do, si, la, sol, fa, mi, re, mi, fa, mi, re, re, do.

109.

Do, re, mi, sol, la, si, do, sol, la, sol, fa, mi, re, mi, re,

do, re, mi, do, mi, fa, sol, mi, fa, sol, la, si, do, si, do.

See if you **can** apply the syllables correctly to the following lessons:

110.

111.

112.

113. This lesson begins with the pitch three. Powers and qualities left to the singers.

mi,   sol,   do.

Mu-sic, mu - sic, heav'nly friend, In thy praise our voic - es blend;

Like the free and bless - ed air, Thou art with us ev - 'ry-where.

114. When all have sung this lesson, divide into two sections and let one sing No. 113 and the other No. 114 together; then change.

do,   mi,

Mu-sic, mu - sic, heav'nly friend, In thy praise our voic - es blend;

do,   fa.

Like the free and bless - ed air, Thou art with us ev - 'ry-where.

Become familiar with singing from the Base Staff, for the third part in this book is almost entirely written upon it. The following lesson is a round for four divisions. The figures 1, 2, 3, 4, show how the divisions commence—2 begins when 1 gets to 2, 3 begins when 2 gets to 2, and 4 begins when 3 gets to 2. Sing " round and round."

115.

Now we drop our slates and pen - cils, Rul-ers, pens, our school u - ten-sils;

Reading, writ - ing, spell - ing, too, Till we've sung our les - son through.

CHAPTER VI.

RESTS.

116. A silence during a piece of music is called a Rest. A silence as long as a quarter note is called a Quarter Rest. A silence as long as a half note is called a Half Rest. The characters that stand for these rests are called *Quarter Rests* and *Half Rests*.

117.

118.

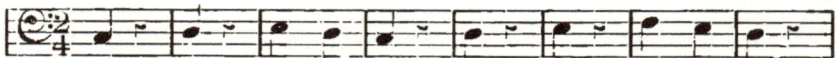

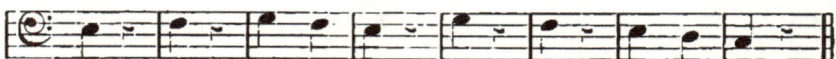

119.

120. The following lesson may be sung as a round by two sections, one commencing one measure after the other.

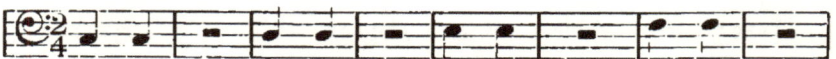

121.

No,   no,   no,   no,   no,   no,   no,   no,

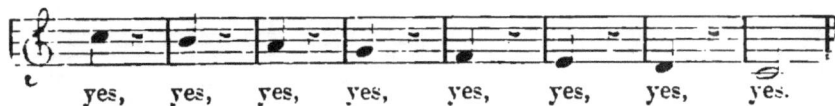

yes,   yes,   yes,   yes,   yes,   yes,   yes,   yes.

122. When all have sung No. 122, sing No. 121 and 122 **together.**

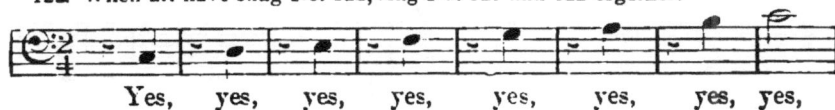

Yes,   yes,   yes,   yes,   yes,   yes,   yes,   yes,

no,   no,   no,   no,   no,   no,   no,   no.

123. The power and quality to be used here are very evident; there is no need of indicating them. Syllables first.

Hark! hark! all a - round! Si-lence keep, make not a sound!

Hush! hush! not a sound! Si-lence keep! make not a sound!

124. *pp*

Hush! hush! do not speak; For in si - lence we must seek.

f

They're found! Re - joice! Give thanks, with cheerful voice.

125.

See! see! rests a-bound; Signs of si-lence. not of sound.

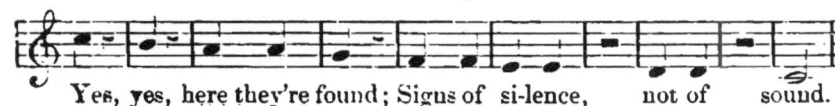

Yes, yes, here they're found; Signs of si-lence, not of sound.

Hark! hark! hark!

Somber tone. The power marks are right here, excepting for the last line of second verse. What power and quality should that have? The *tie*, near the end, makes the two half notes stand for one tone four beats long.

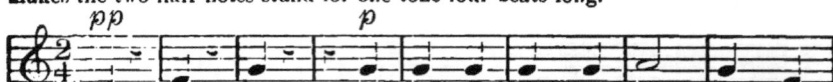

1. Hark! hark! hark!   The wea - ry winds are sigh - ing, The
2. Hark! hark! hark!   More chill the streams are flow - ing, More
3. Hark! hark! hark!   Where hap - py ones were sing - ing, A

with-ered leaves are   fly - ing, The sum-mer time is dy - ing.
swift the wings are   go - ing, Where sun-ny skies are glow - ing.
thou-sand knells are   ring - ing, Their sad-ness to us bring - ing.

Always Truth.

You will be inclined to sing this a little faster than the previous song. Bold quality and a pretty loud power.

1. Truth, truth,   al - ways truth! Let no lie de - file thy youth;
2. Truth, truth,   hon - est, sure, Truth is strong and must en - dure;
3. Truth, truth,   al - ways truth! Let no lie de - file thy youth;

If thou'rt wrong be thine the shame, Speak the truth, and bear the blame.
Falsehood lasts a short, short day, Then it van - ish - es a - way.
Truth is might - y, sure and fast, Cer - tain to pre - vail at last.

CHAPTER VII.

TRIPLE MEASURE, DOTTED HALF NOTE AND REST, MOVEMENT.

126. When music is of such a nature that it makes beats group themselves into *threes*, it is said to be in *Triple* measure. The motions of the hand are down, left, up.

127. The first beat in each measure is more prominent in the mind than the others, and is called the *Accented beat*. The others are *Unaccented beats*.

128. A length as long as three quarters is called a *Dotted Half*, and is represented by a *Dotted half note*.

129. The figure 3 stands for triple measure. Beat-note as before. (Practice beating triple measure before singing these lessons.)

130.

do,   re,   mi,   fa,   sol,   la,

si,   do,   do, si, la, sol,   fa, mi, re, do.

131. Sing the lesson with syllables until it goes smoothly. Do not beat time faster at the dotted half lengths.

Homeward we row, Stead - y and slow, Sing as we ride

O'er the blue tide; Homeward we row, Stead - y and slow.

132. Syllables first.

Hear ye the song Float - ing a - long! What does it say?

Let us be gay. What does it say? Let us be gay.

133. Do not forget absolute and relative naming.

do, mi, sol, do, sol, do,

sol, do, sol, mi, do.

134.

135. Perfect all these lessons with syllables, beating time. It will be an excellent plan to form the habit of examining the words to see what powers and qualities should be used.

Come to the greenwood, so cool and so fair, Beau-ty and gladness will

wel-come us there, Beau-ty and glad-ness will wel-come us there.

136. When this has been sung, sing 135 and 136 together.

Come to the greenwood, so cool and so fair, Beau-ty and gladness will

wel-come us there, Beau-ty and glad-ness will wel-come us there.

137. Introduce *Dotted half rest.*

Now we will sing till the old win-dows shake,

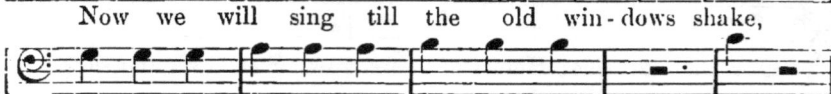

But let's be sure that we make no mis - - - take,

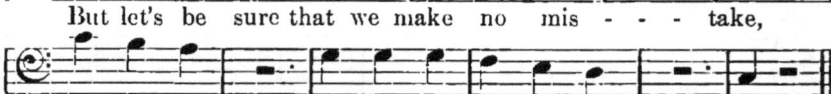

Yes, let's be sure that we make no mis - - take.

Dare to be Right.

Name pitches (letter and numeral names). Syllables first.

1. Dare to be right! Dare to be true! Each has a work that no
2. Dare to be right! Dare to be true! Faults in an - oth - er will
3. Dare to be right! Dare to be true! Keep a bright manhood for-

oth - er can do; Yes, each has a work that no oth-er can do.
nev-er save you; No, faults in an - oth - er will nev-er save you.
ev - er in view; Yes, keep a bright manhood for - ev - er in view.

138. The speed at which a piece of music should go is called its *Movement.*

139. The movement we have been singing in so far, is called *Moderato.* (We have sung a little faster than *Moderato* once or twice.)

140. The next piece should go a little faster than *Moderato*, and the movement mark for that is *Allegretto.*

141.
Allegretto.

I know that you know that we know that they know that

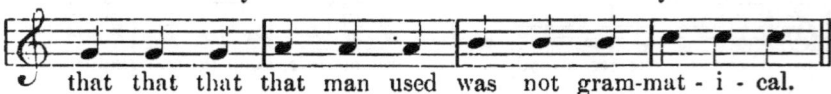

that that that that man used was not gram-mat - i - cal.

NOTE.—Will the teacher allow the writer to give his idea here, more fully, on the subject of movement? *Moderato* seems to take the place among movements that "mezzo" does among powers; it is the *medium*—neither fast nor slow. On one side of *moderato* is *allegretto*, which is moderately fast; on the other side is *andantino*, which is moderately slow; then comes *allegro*, fast; *andante*, slow, etc. There is generally something in a piece which shows how fast or slow it ought to go—in other words, what its "movement" should be, and it is a good plan to let the class find that out for themselves. Take the following piece for instance, and after it is learned try it with various movements, beginning perhaps with *adagio* (very slow), then try it *andante*, then *andantino*, then *moderato*, then *allegretto*, then *allegro*, and perhaps *presto* (very fast). The writer thinks it would sound best about *allegretto*. At any rate, that is what he would mark it. Movements, like Powers and Qualities, need not always be marked, but can often be left to the discretion or taste of the performer. So far we have been singing mostly *moderato.*

Quickly Arise.

This song will sound best about *Allegro* (pronounced *al-lay-grow*.)

Allegro.

1. Quick-ly a - rise! Quick-ly a - rise! For now the sun-shine is
2. Haste ye a - way! Haste ye a - way! For it is com - ing, the

gild - ing the skies. Quick-ly a - rise! Quick-ly a - rise!
beau - ti - ful day. Beau - ti - ful day! Beau - ti - ful day!

Slowly Sounding.

This song will sound best about *Andante.*

Andante.

1. Slow - ly sounding a - long the dell, Hear the tones of the eve - ning
2. Soft - ly trill-eth a child-ish lay, Birds and bees 'mid the blos - soms

bell, Rest from la - bor its num-bers tell, Its plain-tive numbers tell.
gay; These we heard when the morn was grey, A sim - ple, bird-like lay.

CHAPTER VIII.

QUADRUPLE MEASURE, WHOLE NOTE AND REST.

142. When beats group themselves into *fours*, they make *Quadruple Measure.*
Motions of the hand, down, left, right, up. The first and third beats in quadruple
measure are accented. A length as long as four quarters, or two halves, is called a
Whole, and is represented by a *Whole Note.* The figure 4 stands for quadruple
measure. Beat-note as before.

143. *Moderato.* Practice "beating time" before singing this lesson, then apply
syllables first.

Greet with pleasure this new measure, Mind the ac-cents well;

Firm and stead-y, Are you read - y This long tone to swell?

144. Hold the whole notes their full value. What do the words call for, a loud
power or a soft power—a joyful quality or a somber quality?

do, la,
Roll the tones a - long On the tide of song,

do, sol.
Freight-ed with the joy-ous mu - sic Of our hap-py throng.

145. Keep absolute and relative names of pitches in mind.

146. Learn these lessons thoroughly. Vary power.

147.

148.

149.

150. Introduce *Crescendo* and its abbreviations.

Spring is com-ing   in her beau-ty, Win-ter cold is   o'er;

Welcome, welcome, birds and flow-ers, Welcome back once more.

151. When this has been learned by all, sing 150 and 151 together.
Allegretto.

Spring is **com-ing**   in h r beau-ty. Win-ter cold is   o'er;

Welcome, welcome, birds and flow-ers, Welcome back once more.

152. Introduce *Whole Rest.* The whole rest is used as a measure rest in any kind of measure.

Who will make the first mis-take? Who will make the next?

Who will sing in - to the rest? Who will then be vexed?

Who will make the first mis-take? Who will make the next?

Who will sing in - to the rest? Who will then be vexed?

Come and Join Us.

Moderato.

1. Come and join us, dear com-pan-ions, Come and join our happy throng;
2. Joy is hov-'ring o'er the val-ley, Rush-ing in the wa-ter-falls;
3. Come and praise the lov-ing Fa-ther, For these joys so free-ly giv'n;

Here we'll blend our hearts and voic-es, In the dear delights of song.
Joy in ev-'ry heart is grow-ing, That with-in our cir-cle calls.
So may all our earth-ly pleas-ures Fit us for the joys of heav'n.

Do It.

Syllables first. Take breath well. Speak distinctly.

m **Allegretto.** **Cres.**

1. When your stud-y waits for you, With so-ber judgment view it; And
2. Sloth says false-ly, "by and by You can as well re-new it;" But
3. Fear not tri-als in the way, Nor faint if thorns bestrew it; But

m **Cres.**

nev-er i-dly wish it done, But come at once and do it.
pres-ent strength is sur-est strength, Be-gin at once and do it.
brave-ly try, and strength will come, Be-gin at once and do it.

Kindness.

Beginning on last beat in measure.

Andantino.

1. How soft - ly on the bruis-ed heart A word of kind-ness falls,
2. The weak-est and the poor-est may The sim - ple pit-tance give,
3. As stars up - on the tran-quil sea In mim-ic glo - ry shine,

And to the dry and parch-ed soul, The moist'ning tear-drop calls.
And bid de - light to with-ered hearts Re - turn a gain and live.
So words of kind - ness in the heart, Re - flect the source di - vine.

CHAPTER IX.

SEXTUPLE MEASURE, DOTTED WHOLE.

153. When beats group themselves into *sixes*, they make *Sextuple Measure.* Motions of the hand, down, left, left, right, up, up. Accented beats, first and fourth. These are the best motions for beating time in sextuple measure, for they bring the accented motions as in quadruple.

154. A length as long as six quarters is called a *Dotted Whole*, and represented by a *Dotted Whole Note.* The figure 6 stands for Sextuple Measure. Beat-note as before.

Sing the following lessons with syllables, beating time:

155.

156.

157.

158.

159

160.

161.

162.

163.

164. Moderato.

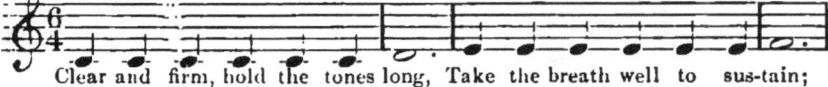

Clear and firm, hold the tones long, Take the breath well to sus-tain;

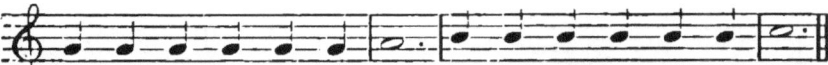

Strive in each line of the song, Time and good tune to main-tain.

165. When this has been learned by all, 164 and 165 may be sung together.
Moderato.

do, mi, fa, sol, do, re,
Clear and firm, hold the tones long, Take the breath well to sus-tain;

mi, fa, sol, do.
Strive in each line of the song, Time and good tune to main-tain.

166. It is difficult to sing sextuple measure *allegretto* and beat six beats in the measure, but you are strongly recommended to work at it until it is thoroughly done. Will the teacher explain *Repeat!*
Allegretto.

{ Glad let our voic-es be, Give them out cheer-ful-ly,
{ Mu-si-cal treas-ure this Sex-tu-ple meas-ure is,

Give them out cheer-ful and strong; } Tripping a-long, Dancing a-long.
Trip-ping and danc-ing a-long, }

167. Introduce tone just below key-tone, with its names and syllables. Nos. 166 and 167 may be sung together.
Allegretto.

{ Glad let our voic-es be, Give them out cheer-ful-ly,
{ Mu-si-cal treas-ure this Sex-tu-ple meas-ure is,

Give them out cheer-ful and strong; } Tripping a-long, Dancing a-long.
Trip-ping and danc-ing a-long,

Joy and Mirth.

Bright tone. Medium power.

1. We're com - ing, we're com - ing from wood - land and hill;
2. For we are the spir - its of joy and of mirth;

We're com - ing, we're com - ing from brook - let and rill;
We dwell in the smiles of this beau - ti - ful earth;

We'll join in your play, and we'll join in your song,
And when we are want - ed we're read - y to come,

We'll join in what - e'er you do all the day long.
To light - en each heart and to bright - en each home.

NOTE—'There is comparatively little music now sung in sextuple measure. Compound double measure generally takes its place. This will be introduced in due time.

CHAPTER X.

KEY, KEY CHARACTERISTICS, HIGHER AND LOWER TONES, SOPRANO, ALTO, TENOR, BASE.

168. The tones we have been singing make a family called a *Key*. **A key is a** family of related tones.

169. The tone in a key that makes the best ending or home tone is called the *Key-tone.*

170. The key-tone of a key is always one or eight. The tone next above key-tone is *two*, the next *three*, and so on up to *eight*. The tone next below key-tone is *seven*, the next *six*, the next *five*, and so on down to *one*. The same key-tone is some-times one and sometimes eight. It is called one when going upward from it. It is called eight when going downward from it. Every one, and every eight, may be a key-tone.

171. It is an interesting fact that every member of this tone-family (key) has its own peculiar character or mental effect. "Key-tone," "one," or "eight," has firm-ness and repose. It is the home tone and the best pitch of all the key to end with. "Two" is a good connecting tone—has boldness, but no repose. "Three" is more gentle or plaintive, with some repose; "four," bold, without repose; "five," bold (dominant), with repose; "six," plaintive, without repose; and "seven," most restless of all—an excellent leading and connecting tone.

172. These different effects, more or less consciously in the minds of singers, are what really enable them to sing the different pitches of a key when they are called for, or when their signs are seen.

173. Syllables help to fix these characteristics in the mind. With "do," we feel the key-tone effect, with "re" that of the bold but restless "two," with "mi" the plaintive "three," and so on.

174. Tone characteristics in a key illustrated.

Moderato.

Do, re, mi, fa, sol, la, si, do, si, la, sol, fa, mi, re, do,

With the tones just sung in mind, C is home we clear - ly find.

Now one step, and dwell on two, For re - pose this will not do;

But with gen - tle, plain-tive three We may rest quite peace-ful - ly.

Rest - ful now the tones no more, While we sing the full, strong four;

But we'll find when we ar - rive, There is strength and rest in five.

Hark! on rest - less breez - es borne, How the plain-tive six doth mourn;

Next is seven, but do not wait, Hur - ry on and get to eight.

175. The tones of a key, from one key-tone to the next key-tone in the order of their names, make what is called the *Scale*. One, two, three, four, five, six, seven, eight, make the *Ascending Scale*, and eight, seven, six, five, four, three, two, one, the *Descending Scale*. In any other order the tones of the key are not the scale, and should not be called tones of the scale, but may always be called tones of the key.

176. The *eight* that we have been singing may be considered *one*, and tones above it used.

177. The *one* that we have been singing may be considered *eight*, and tones below it used.

178. The treble staff must be enlarged to represent lower tones, and the base staff must be enlarged to represent higher tones, than we have been singing.

179. The voices that sing the higher tones easily are Soprano or Treble voices, and those that sing the lower tones easily, Alto voices; but all should sing both parts for practice. Most boys' voices should sing Alto, or, in this book, the third part, often written on the base staff.

180. Sing only the pitches that you can reach easily. Stop when they get too high or too low.

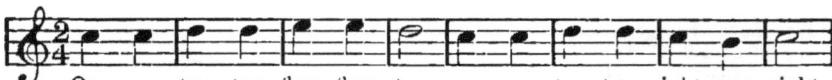

One, one, two. two, three, three, two, one, one, two, two, eight, seven, eight,
do, do, re, re, mi, mi, re, do, do, re, re, do,. si, do,

eight, eight, seven, seven, six, six, five, one, one, two, two, three, two, one.
do, do, si, si, do, do, sol, do, do, re, re, mi, re, do.

181. In going up from key-tone, the key-tone is considered as one; in going down from key-tone, it is considered as eight.

One, one, two, two, three, three, two, one, one, two, two, eight, seven, eight,
do, do, re, re, mi, mi, re, do, do, re, re, do, si, do,

eight, eight, seven, seven, six, six, five, one, one, two, two, three, two, one.
do, do, si, si, la, la, sol, do, do, re, re, mi, re, do.

182.

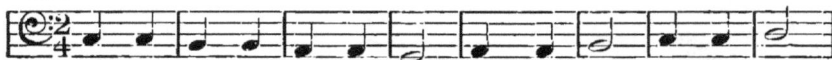

do, do, si, si, la, la, sol, la, la, si, do, do, re,
In the for-est, dark and deep, 'Neath the trees, Loft-y trees,

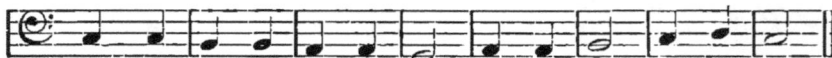

do, do, si, si, la, la, sol, la, la, si, do, re, do.
Where the shad-ows soft-ly creep, Sighs the breeze, Summer breeze.

183. Soprano sing the upper part of this lesson, and Alto lower.

do, do, re, re, mi, mi, re, do, do, si, si, la, si, do,
Gladness, glad-ness ev-'rywhere, In the earth and in the air;

do, do, re, re, mi, mi, re, do, do, re, re, do, si, do.
Glad-ness in the swell-ing song. Gladness in the hap-py throng.

184. From one key-tone to the next one above or below is said to be an *Octave*. It is also an Octave from any two (re) to the next two above or below, or from any three (mi) to the next, and so of all pitches. Tones an Octave apart have the same names, both absolute and relative, and the same syllables.

Sing these lessons with syllables, first each part separately, then both parts together.

185.

186. What kind of measure?

187.

188.

Who are These?

Name pitches, and all sing each part first.

m **Allegretto.**

1. Who are these with steps so free? Who are these with voice of glee?
2. Come, then, come, ye peo - ple near, Ga - ther round the shrine so dear;
3. All to - geth - er let us sing, Trib - ute glad to mu - sic bring,

f

Sons of song, and daughters, we, That make this com - pa - ny.
Join with us and do not fear, For ye are wel - come here.
And our song on joy - ful wing Up to the heaven's shall ring.

Do Your Best.

Words show power and quality.

Moderato.

1. All a-long the for-est dim Ris-es one tri-umph-al hymn;
2. Bird and flow'r and mountain stream, In the sunlight glance and gleam:
3. Then, my neigh-bor, let us see, Tho' we may not might-y be,

With his proud-ly swell-ing breast Ev-'ry song-ster does his best.
North and south and east and west, Small and great all do their best.
That we keep high heav'n's be-hest, And in all things do our best.

Clear Echo is Sounding.

Question in regard to measure.

m **Moderato.**   *f*   *pp*   *m*

1. Clear ech-o is sounding, Hurrah! hurrah!
   From hillside rebounding, Hurrah! hurrah! } The bright birds are winging, The
2. The brooklet is danc-ing, Hurrah! hurrah!
   The sunbeams are glancing, Hurrah! hurrah! } The green leaves are o'er us, The

f   *pp*

woodlands are ring-ing, All join in our sing-ing, Hur-rah! hur-rah!
hill-side be-fore us, To ech-o our cho-rus, Hur-rah! hur-rah!

Sunshine.

In one place in the Alto two pitches are sung to one syllable. This is indicated by a curved line, called a *Slur*. Pronounce "merrily" as if it were spelled merry-ly. Do not give the sound of "u" in "rush" to the second syllable.

Allegretto.

1. Smil-ing in the val-ley, Streaming o'er the plain;
   See the mer-ry sunshine Bring-ing joy a-gain; } Struggling thro' the branches
2. Ting-ing ev-'ry bil-low, Roll-ing on the sea;
   Mak-ing all so gladsome, Woodland, lake and lea; } Welcom'd by the song-sters
3. Mer-ry, mer-ry sun-light, Gleaming from the West,
   Of all Nature's beau-ties, Thee I love the best; } By our heav'nly Fa-ther,

Of the for-est tree, Danc-ing on the stream-let, Glid-ing mer-ri-ly.
In each sha-dy glen, As soft lines it tra-ces With a gold-en pen.
Sent us from a-bove; Shall we not re-ceive it, Mes-sen-ger of love?

Angel Voices. (Christmas Song.)

Introduce eighth notes, two to a beat. Practice each part first all together. Words show power and quality.

Moderato.

1. An - gel voic - es, an - gel voic - es, sounding thro' the air;
2. O - pen wide and let them in, these shin-ing ones of song;
3. An - gel voic - es, an - gel voic - es, from the realms a - bove;

Glo - ry! glo - ry! how they sing their glad-ness ev - 'ry-where,
Heav'nly love and bless - ed - ness with - in their ranks be - long.
Ev - er may we hear their songs, so full of hope and love;

"Peace, good will for ev - er more to all man-kind," they cry,
All may share their wondrous joy, who ope to them the door,
In the field, the shop, the mart, the school-room and the hall,

An - gel voic - es, an - gel voic - es, sound-ing thro' the sky.
In the cot-tage, in the hall, in homes of rich or poor.
Bless-ing us while bless - ing Him whose care is o'er us all.

THROUGH THE KEYS.

REMARKS TO THE TEACHER.—While the author of this work leaves every teacher free to pursue his own course, he begs leave to offer the following ideas:

ABSOLUTE AND RELATIVE PITCH NAMES.

We can speak of a tone by its *length name* (whole, half, quarter, etc.), or by its *power name* (mezzo, piano, forte, etc.), or by its *quality name* (joyful, sad, sweet, sympathetic, etc.), but it is its *pitch name* which is most important, because it is by *pitches* that melodies and harmonies are made. Every musical pitch has a fixed name, but that does not prevent its having other names to describe different uses that it may be put to: just as every person has an absolute or fixed name, and then other names to describe the situations or relations in which he may be placed. For instance, "James Reed" (absolute name), in his school may be "monitor," in his literary society, "chairman," in his ball-club, "first base," in his father's store, "book-keeper," at home, "son," "brother," etc. These are his *relative names*, because they describe the relationships he holds to other people in these different ways.

So with tone-pitches :—C (fixed or absolute name), may be so surrounded that it will be "key-tone" or "do," or it may be so related that it will be "five," or "sol," (or "dominant," as it would be called in studying harmony ;) or in another connection the same individual may be "leading tone," or "seven,"—and it may have many other situations. All these names,—one, two, three, etc., do, re, mi, etc., tonic, dominant, etc., are the *relative names* of tone-pitches, because they show or describe their relationship to other tones. C, or G, is fixed, unchangeable and independent. It has that name, whether it is connected with any other tones or not, but neither C nor G nor any other absolute pitch can have the "home" or "key-tone" sound of "one," nor the boldness of the dominant "five," nor the restlessness of the "leading" "seven," nor any other characteristics described by these relative names, until it is connected with other tones.

FORMING OTHER KEYS AFTER SINGING IN THE KEY OF C.

The class have been singing the tone-pitches C, D, E, F, G, A, and B, in scales and tunes, and have always found that they made C the home or key-tone.

Now substitute F sharp for F (omitting F entirely), but keep the other tones used in the key of C. Let the class sing them in scale or tune form, and G will be key-tone. It will be key-tone, not because the teacher says so, nor because some calculation has shown that it ought to be so, but because the class *feel* that it is so,—they hear that G is now home just as they heard that C was, in the key of C.

As G is now key-tone, the new key is called the key of G.

There is no need of studying intervals here, it is only necessary to show what tones make the new key. When this is done the class see that the key of G has one pitch that the key of C has not, and that using F sharp instead of F makes a change in the character of all the other tone they have been using. They hear that C has no longer the home or key-tone sound, but the very different effect of four or "fa,"—G, instead of being five is one, etc. A knowledge of intervals here would not explain this change in the mental effect of these tones, and would embarrass and delay the class.

Having sung some tones of this new key from dictation, applying "do" to one, " re" to two etc., we are ready to prepare the staffs to represent the new key. The staff, as we have been using it, stands for the key of C,—no line or space of it stands for the new tone F sharp, but some of the lines and spaces do stand for F, and that pitch we do not use. To make the staff stand for the new key, we take the degrees that stand for F (that we do not want), and make them stand for F sharp (that we do want). This is done by a character called a sharp, thus (teacher place a sharp on fifth line of treble staff). The sharp thus used not only affects the degree on which it is placed, but all the octaves above and below it on the same staff.

[Any who would be interested to see the author's mode of giving this lesson are referred the Normal Musical Hand-book, page 150.]

To introduce the key of D, keep all the tones of the key of G, excepting C,—omit that,—use C sharp instead, and D will be found to be key-tone. By using, of course, is meant, singing. The teacher sings in the key of G, the class naming the absolute pitches as they hear them Then, when they hear C sharp, they realize that a new pitch has been introduced, and after the have sung it, they have all the material for the new family.

TRANSPOSITION.

Forming new keys and singing in them is sometimes called "Transposition," but there need be no transposition in introducing a new key, and generally there is none. Transposition i singing, playing, or writing a particular piece of music higher or lower, that is, in another key but it must be the same piece. Singing one piece or exercise in one key, and then a differ n exercise or piece in another key, is not transposition, and that is what is generally done i forming new keys. A key can not be transposed any more than an absolute pitch can be. Both are fixed and immovable.

The misunderstanding on this subject comes first, from giving to the word "scale" some thing of the meaning of "key," and second, from the fact that singing the scale in one key and then singing it in another is transposition. But the teacher does not sing the scale in the new key until he has formed it. Other exercises of less range than the scale come first in the proper order of teaching.

Practically, one of the easiest things in the singing-class is transposition ; it is but singing an exercise or a piece higher or lower. It can be done just as soon as the class can sing anything but the theory of transposition, or rather the representation of it on the board, is not easy until many other things have been done. In the writer's opinion, a class should practice in all the keys before touching the subject of transposition theoretically.

SIGNATURE.

The meaning of this word is "sign of key." In looking at a piece of music, if you can tell what key it is in, it has a "sign of key." That is self-evident. The arrangement of a staff by which it is made to represent a key, constitutes this sign.

Arranging the staff to represent a key is done just at the right of the clef in the "signature place," and there musicians look to see what key the staff is arranged for, and there they find a "sign of key" for every key in music. If a musician could not tell what key a piece of music was in, unless there were sharps or flats in the signature place, then they alone would constitute "signs of keys." If, however, he can tell what key a piece of music is in, when there are no sharps or flats in the signature place, then something else besides sharps and flats become "signs of keys,"—that also is self-evident.

The musician looks at all the lines and spaces in the signature place to see what key the staff is prepared for, and he always finds them in one of three conditions, viz.: sharped, flatted, or natural, and either condition is a sign to him. Also, there is a name for every combination that is made there, and this name, or its abbreviation, is the name of "sign of key," or signature, there found.

Without much thought one might suppose that it is only necessary to see one sharp in the signature place in order to know that the staff is prepared for the key of G, and that therefore "one sharp" is the whole name of the sign or signature of that key. But conceal all but the upper line in the signature place and no one can tell with certainty that the staff is prepared for the key of G, although the "one sharp" may be in plain sight. Every line and space must be seen, and must be seen to be properly sharped or natural, or there is no certain signature The natural degrees are as important in representing the pitches of the key as are the sharped ones.

Therefore, saying that "one sharp" is the signature of the key of G, is an abbreviation. The whole statement is,—"one degree sharped and all the rest not affected by that sharp, natural."

The whole statement of the arrangement of the staff for the key of D would be " two degrees sharped and all the rest not affected by those sharps, natural." This, in common parlance, is properly abbreviated to " two sharps."

The arrangement of the staff to represent the key of C is to have all the degrees natural. The abbreviation of this is simply " natural."

KEY OF G.

189. Introduce F-sharp. Drop F as soon as F-sharp is recognized and sung. Sing the pitches of this family (F-sharp, G, A, B, C, D and E) until the class realize that G is key-tone.

190. Sing the following lesson. We begin with the pitches that we are familiar with, and when we arrive at the pitch that is to be the new key-tone we apply to it the syllable "do," and then sing in the new key.

C, D, E, F, G, G, G, G, G, F-sharp, G, A, B, B, B, B.
do, re, mi, fa, sol, sol, sol, sol, do,   si,   do, re, mi, mi, mi, mi.

B, A, G, F-sharp, E, D, E, F-sharp, G, A, B, A, G.
mi, re, do,   si,   la, sol, la,   si,   do, re, mi, re, do.

191. Let us make the staff represent these pitches. There is no F in the key of *g*, therefore the staff must not represent F. There is F-sharp, therefore the staff must represent it. This is easily done. Place a character called a sharp upon one of the degrees that stand for F, and it will stop the staff from representing F and make it represent F-sharp. The sharp so placed affects the octave above or below it.

NOTE.—At the commencement of each key, its pitches will be represented in scale form—not for practice, (we begin with something easier,) but to show who are its members, together with their names and location (so to speak) upon the staffs, (Treble and Base.)

192. Scales in the key of G.

Absolute. G, A, B, C, D, E, F♯, G, F♯, E, D, C, B, A, G.
Relative. 1, 2, 3, 4, 5, 6, 7, 8, 7, 6, 5, 4, 3, 2, 1.

Absolute. G, A, B, C, D, E, F♯, G, F♯, E, D, C, B, A, G.
Relative. 1, 2, 3, 4, 5, 6, 7, 8, 7, 6, 5, 4, 3, 2, 1.

193. Call key-tone one when tones go *up* from it; call it eight when tones go *down* from it. Name pitches absolutely and relatively.

do, do, re, re, mi, mi, re, mi, mi, fa, fa, mi, re, do,
Now with voic-es full and free, Sing we in the key of G;

do, do, si, si, la, la, sol, do, sol, la, la, si, si, do.
G, G, F-sharp, E and D, Just as eas-y this, as C.

194. All practice from the base clef.

do, si, la, sol, sol, la, si, do, do, re, mi, re,
No-tice in base, Key-tone, this space; 'Twill not be long

fa, mi, re, mi, do, si, la, sol, la, si, do, mi, re, do.
Ere in our song All a-bout this key to us will be-long.

195. Name pitches, absolute and relative. Increase ascending, diminish descending.

do,   re,   mi,   fa,   sol, fa, mi, re, do, si, do.

196.

do,   si,   la,   sol, sol,   la, si, do, re, do.

197.

do, si, la, sol, la, si, do, re, mi, fa,   mi,   re,   do.

198.

do, sol, do, mi,   sol,   fa, mi, re,   do, sol, do, mi,

sol, fa, mi, re, do.

199.

do,   si,   do,   sol,   fa,   mi,   fa,   sol, do.

Harp of Freedom.

Soprano.

do, do,   re,   re,

1. Harp of Free-dom, wake the song! Pour its glorious mu - sic forth,
2. Harp of Free-dom, wake the song! Tuneful be each quiv'ring string,

Alto.

do, do, sol, sol,

A - ges shall its tones prolong, Round and round the list'ning earth.
Let thy numbers, high and strong, Reach to heav'n's eter-nal King.

Sunlight.

Give relative and absolute names. Let the different parts come in without losing the beat. Be sure and sing syllables, each part alone first, in all these lessons.

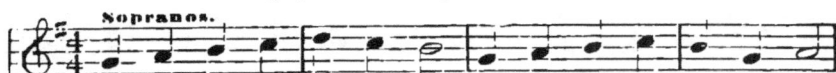

Sunlight, sunlight pure and fair, Gilds the up-lands, vale and lea;

Life and love are ev-'ry-where, And joy for you and me.

Down the hill the brook is dancing, Crystal waters brightly glancing,

To the riv-er swift ad-vancing, Beauti-ful to see.

Sing prelude again before singing second verse.

1. Sun-light, sun-light free and fair, Gilds the uplands, vale and lea;
2. Down the hill the brooklets dance, See their wa-ters brightly glance,

Life and love are ev-'ry-where, And joy for you and me.
To the riv-er they ad-vance, Most beauti-ful to see.

Morning Papers. (Round for Three Divisions.)

sol,   re,   mi,
Morn-ing   pa-pers, morn-ing   pa-pers, All the ri-ots,

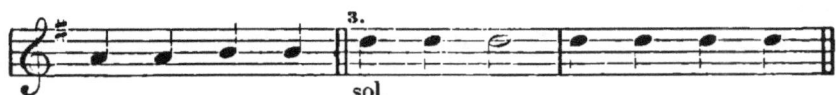

sol,
rows and   ca-pers, Trib-une, Times, In-ter-O-cean.

Swinging Low.

Syllables first.   Each part separate.

Moderato.

1. Swinging low, To and fro, See the May-bells' rud-dy glow,
2. Swinging low, To and fro, Where the sum-mer breez-es blow,

Ring - ing out their mer-ry chime, Where sweetest flow - ers grow.
Rob - in joins his mer - ry song, In ac - cents sweet and low.

Sleighing Song.

Syllables first.   Produce the echo effect, where it is marked alternately loud and very soft.

Allegretto.

1. The diamonds gleam in the sun's bright beam, As mer - ri - ly forth we go;
2. Our sleighbells sing with a silv'ry ring, A mel - o - dy well we know;
3. The trees fly past, and the wint'ry blast With i - ci-cle breath may blow;

With eyes whose light from the heart is bright, As we ride o'er the pure white snow
Our steeds keep time to the mer-ry chime, As we dance o'er the field of snow.
From fur's warm fold de - fy the cold, As we glide o'er the clear white snow

Yo, ho! yo, ho! yo, ho! yo, ho! As we ride o'er the pure white snow.
Yo, ho! yo, ho! yo, ho! yo, ho! As we dance o'er the field of snow.
Yo, ho! yo, ho! yo, ho! yo, ho! As we glide o'er the clear white snow.

THE KEY OF D.

200. Introduce the key of D. There is no F nor C in this key, but F sharp and C sharp instead.

201. It would be well to practice the pitches of his key by calling for them before singing the following lessons.

202. In the following lesson we begin in the key of G, and when we come to the new key-tone apply "do" to it, and then go on singing in the new key. Sing this lesson slowly.

G, G, F sharp, E, D, D, D, D, D, E, F sharp, G, A, A, A, A.
do, do, si, la, sol, sol, sol, sol, do, re, mi, fa, sol, sol, sol, sol.

A, B, C sharp, D, C sharp, B, A, G, F sharp, E, D, C sharp, D.
sol, la, si, do, si, la, sol, fa, mi, re, do, si, do.

203. Arrange the staff so that it will stand for all the pitches of this key. See that the staff does not represent either F, or C, for neither of those pitches belong to this key.

204. Tones of the key of D, in scale form.

Absolute. D, E, F♯, G, A, B, C♯, D, C♯, B, A, G, F♯, E, D.

Relative. 1, 2, 3, 4, 5, 6, 7, 8, 7, 6, 5, 4, 3, 2, 1.

Absolute. D, E, F♯, G, A, B, C♯, D, C♯, B, A, G, F♯, E, D.

Relative. 1, 2, 3, 4, 5, 6, 7, 8, 7, 6, 5, 4, 3, 2, 1.

205. Name pitches before singing. Key-tone is sometimes one and sometimes eight.

do, do, re, re, mi, mi, fa, mi, mi, fa, fa, sol, sol, la,

While we sing in this new key, Do we sing the pitch named C?

do, do, si, la, sol, fa, mi, re, re, do, do, si, si, do.

No, just list, and 'twill be clear, 'Tis not C, but C sharp here.

206. At the last part of this lesson the sopranos sing the upper tones of the octave, and the altos the lower.

do, do, do, si, la, la, la, sol, do, re, mi, fa,

Third line of base Is key-tone place, When four is G,

sol, sol, sol, do, do, re, mi, fa, sol, la, sol, sol, sol, do.

And home is D, When four is G, And when home tone is D.

207. Make thorough work of applying syllables in this new way. *Moderato* when not otherwise marked.

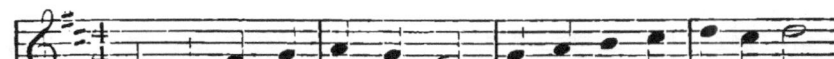

Do, re, mi, fa, sol, fa, mi, fa, sol, la, si, do, si, do,

do, si, la, sol, fa, mi, re, si, la, sol, fa, mi, re, do.

208.

Do, mi, sol, mi, do, re, mi, re, do, sol, do, mi,

sol, mi, do, mi, sol, fa, mi, re, mi, re, do, sol, do.

209. Question continually in regard to measure, pitches, etc.

Do, re, mi, fa, do, mi, sol,

do, mi, sol, do, sol, mi, do,

How the Chorus.

Each part first. Words show plainly power and quality.

mi, re, do, do, si, la, sol, fa, mi, re, do, fa, mi, re,
1. How the cho-rus sweeps a - long, In the glorious march of song;
2. Swelling high, the anthem grand Ris - es up from ev - 'ry land;

do, re, mi, mi, fa, fa, mi, re, mi, fa, mi, re, do, sol,

mi, re, do, do, si, la, sol, fa, mi, re, la, sol, sol, do.
Sweeter praise than earth can sing, From each grateful heart doth spring.
Thro' the sound-ing arch a - bove Rolls the hymn of joy and love.

do, re, mi, mi, fa, fa, mi, re, mi, fa, fa, mi, sol, do.

To Ope their Trunks. (Round in Three Parts.)

Syllables first.

1.

To ope their trunks the trees are nev - er seen, How

3.

then do they get on their robes of green? *They leave them out.*

Spring is Coming.

Name the pitches before singing, and sing the syllables first.

Sopranos.

Spring is com-ing, spring is com-ing, Hear the woodlands ring!

Altos.

Spring is com-ing, spring is com-ing, Answ'ring back we sing;

Sopranos.

Skies are bright and hearts are light, While pleasure crowns the day.

Altos, from Base staff.

Win-ter drear we no more fear, So wel-come back the May.

Sing prelude again for second verse.

CHORUS.

1. Spring is com-ing, spring is coming, Hear the merry woodlands ring!
2. Skies are light and hearts are lighter, Joy and pleasure crown the day;

Spring is com-ing, spring is com-ing, Answ'ring back we sing.
Win-ter drear we no more fear, So wel-come back the May.

Johnny. (Round in Four Parts.)

John-ny, John-ny, What! what! So we keep

sing-ing, and so we keep call-ing him.

Music Now is Ringing.

Let the words indicate power and quality.   Explain pause.

Allegretto.

1. Mu - sic   now   is   ring-ing From our cho - rus strong;
2. Lis - ten   to   its   num-bers, Joy - ful - ly   they swell;
3. Still the strains are   ring-ing, Clear, and sweet, and strong;

Join - ing all with cheer-ful voice, The har - mo - ny   pro-long.
Sounding far o'er hill and dale, Of hap - pi - ness they tell.
Hear the joy - ful ech - oes wake, And send us   back our song.

Sweet Sabbath Eve.

With syllables first.

Andantino.

1. Sweet Sabbath eve, bright is thy smile, Linger, oh, linger, to cheer us a - while;
2. Sweet Sabbath eve, hallow'd and blest, Sending the soul to its ha-ven of   rest;
3. Sweet Sabbath eve, bear on thy wing Upward to heaven the praise that we sing;

Sweet Sab-bath eve, beau-ti - ful ray, Fade not so quickly a - way.
Lin - ger a - while, beau-ti - ful ray, Fade not so quickly a - way.
Faint-er thy voice, fad - ed thy hue, Gen-tly we bid thee a - dieu.

Ferryman, Row.

PALMER HARTSOUGH.

210. Introduce *dotted quarter.* When there are six eighths in a measure, and the movement is somewhat fast, it is easier to beat two beats than six,—three eighths or their value to a beat. Such measures are called *Compound Double Measures.* The dotted quarter is really "beat-note."

1. O - ver, o - ver, o - ver, fer - ry - man, fer - ry - man, row.
2. O - ver, o - ver, o - ver, fer - ry - man, fer - ry - man, row.
3. O - ver, o - ver, o - ver, fer - ry - man, fer - ry - man, row.

Petulant spring has swollen the tide; Ferryman, pull! for the river is wide.
August has drank where merry streams flow; Ferryman, pull! for the river is low.
Frozen the wave, and winter is chill; Ferryman, rest! for the river is still.

Ferryman, Row. - Concluded.

O - ver, o - ver, o - ver, Fer - ry - man, fer - ry - man, row.
O - ver, o - ver, o - ver, Fer - ry - man, fer - ry - man, row.
No more o - ver, o - ver, Fer - ry - man, fer - ry - man, row.

KEY OF A.

211. Introduce the key of A. Neither C, F, nor G here, but instead F♯, C♯, and G♯. It is a good plan to have the class appreciate that A is key-tone, before commencing the practice of the written lessons.

212 Sing the following lesson, beginning in the key of D. Change to the key of A in your minds as well as with your voices.

D, E, F♯, G, A, A, A, A, A, G♯, A, B, C♯, C♯, C♯,
do, re, mi, fa, sol, sol, sol, sol, do, si, do, re, mi, mi, mi,

C♯, C♯, B, A, G♯, F♯, E, D, C♯, D, E, F♯, G♯, A.
mi, mi, re, do, si, la, sol, fa, mi, fa, sol, la, si, do.

213. Three degrees of the staff sharped, and all the rest, not affected by those sharps, kept natural, constitutes the arrangement of the staff and consequently the signature for this key.

214. The pitches of the key of A represented in scale form.

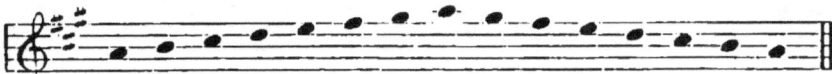

Absolute. A, B, C♯, D, E; F♯, G♯, A, G♯, F♯, E, D, C♯, B, A.
Relative. 1, 2, 3, 4, 5, 6, 7, 8, 7, 6, 5, 4, 3, 2, 1.

Absolute. A, B, C♯, D, E, F♯, G♯, A, G♯, F♯, E, D, C♯, B A.
Relative. 1, 2, 3, 4, 5, 6, 7, 8, 7, 6, 5, 4, 3, 2, 1.

215.

do, do, re, re, mi, mi, re, do, do, si, si, la, si, do,
Key-tone, two and three, three, re, In this fam-i - ly of A;

do, do, re, re, mi, mi, re, do, do, si, la, sol, sol, do.
Keep in mind the key-tone place, In so - pra-no and in base.

216.

do, si, la, sol, la, sol, fa, mi, re, re, re, do, do, do,
Soon we shall be Sure of this key, Read-ing as read-i-ly

fa, fa, fa, mi, la, la, la, sol, sol, sol, do, re, si, do.
Here as in C, Sing-ing as stead-i-ly, Voic-es as free.

217.

Do, si, la, sol, la, si, do, re, mi, re, do, mi, re,   mi, re, do, si,

do, si, la, sol, fa, sol, la, si, do.

218. Measures, pitches, beats, etc.

do,   re.

re, do, re, mi, fa, mi, fa, sol, la.

219.

do, sol, mi,   fa, sol, la, sol,   sol, do, mi,

re, do, re, do,   do, mi, sol, fa, mi, re, do,   si, do.

220. Compound double measure. Dotted quarter the beat-note.

mi,   mi,   re,   mi,   mi,

re,   do,   sol,   fa.

Now the Vail of Evening.

Andantino.

do,   si, la, sol, la, la, sol, fa,   mi,   fa,

1. Now the vail of eve-ning Falls on western skies,   And the sounds of
2. And when silent night dews To the flowers cling,   Ans'ring ev'ry

do,   fa, fa, mi, re, do,   re, mi, fa, sol,

sol, la, re, do, si, do.

twi - light, Echo sweet re-plies,   Echo sweet re - plies.
mur-mur, Still the echoes sing,   Still the echoes sing.

do, mi, fa,   sol,sol, do, replies,yes, fa,   sol,   do.
                            they sing,yes,

Why are the Stars.   (Round in three parts.)

Moderato. (Syllables first.)

Why are the stars the best as-tron-o-mers? Wait! wait!

wait!   Oh, because they have studded the heav'ns for ag-es.

Up and Off.

Sopranos.

Up and off, the sun is ris-ing, Let him not be-hold us here,

Altos.

Up and off, the fields are smil-ing, Ev-'ry bird is sing-ing clear.

Sopranos.

To our la - bor gai - ly stepping, Ev-'ry one our chorus join,

Up and Off. Concluded.

Altos, from base staff.

If the storm comes, we can bear it, If the sun shines, let it shine.

Sing prelude again before singing second verse.

CHORUS.

1. Up and off, the sun is ris-ing, Let him not be-hold us here,
2. To our la-bor gai-ly stepping, Ev-'ry voice the cho-rus join,

Up and off, the fields are smil-ing, Ev-'ry bird is sing-ing clear.
If the storm comes, we can bear it, If the sun shines, let it shine.

Do Your Best.

Moderato.

1. All a-long the for-est dim Ris-es the tri-umphal hymn;
2. Bird and flow'r and mountain stream, In the sunlight glance and gleam;
3. Then, my neighbor, let us see, Tho' we may not mighty be,

With his proud-ly swell-ing breast Ev-'ry song-ster does his best.
North and south and east and west, Small and great all do their best.
That we keep high heav'n's behest, And in all things do our best.

The Land Without a King.

Compound double measure.

1. A glo-ry shout! hurrah! hurrah! Now let the wel-kin ring!
2. Let monarchs reign on thrones of pow'r And to their scep-ters cling,
3. Hurrah! hurrah! the world shall join And songs of free-dom sing,

Hurrah! a hundred years have crown'd The Land without a king.
A hundred years of glo-ry crowns The Land without a king.
Till ev-'ry land like ours shall be, A Land without a king.

Come and Rest.

Syllables and each part first.

1. Come and rest, come and rest, There is   a calm, a   sure re-treat,
2. Come and rest, come and rest, For there is peace our souls may meet
3. Come and rest, come and rest, Oh, may our hearts forget to   beat

'Tis found beneath the mercy seat ; Come and rest, come and rest.
Around the blessed mer-cy seat ; Come and rest, come and rest.
Ere we for-get the mer-cy seat ; Come and rest, come and rest.

Free from Care.

Let words indicate power and quality.   Name pitches.

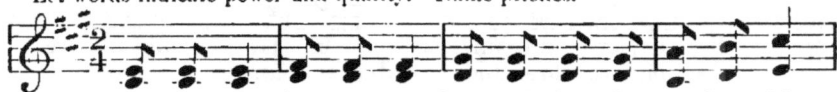

1. Free from care, Light as air, Roam we thro' the meadows fair ;
2. None can tell Half so well How in hap - pi - ness to dwell,

Rest is   sweet, And a   treat, When the work's complete.
As   can they Who each day Work be - fore they play.

CHORUS.

Hap-py, hap-py let us be, Stud-y's o - ver, we are free,

Work is done, play's be - gun, Hap-py let   us be.

KEY OF E.

221. The tones F♯, G♯, A, B, C♯ and D♯ cluster about E as key-tone. D is the tone omitted, and D♯ the new tone to be introduced.

222. Sing the following lesson, which begins in the key of A and leads into the new key:

A, A, G♯, F♯, E, E, E, E, E, D♯, E, F♯, G♯, G♯, G♯, G♯, G♯, F♯, G♯ A,
do, do, si, la, sol, sol, sol, sol, do, si, do, re, mi, mi, mi, mi, mi, re, mi, fa,

B, B, B, B, C♯, B, A, G♯, F♯, E, D♯, C♯, B, B, C♯, D♯, E.
sol, sol, sol, sol, la, sol, fa, mi, re, do, si, la, sol, sol, la, si, do.

223. To make the staff represent the pitches of this key, four sharps must be used. Pitches of this key in scale form.

Absolute. E, F♯, G♯, A, B, C♯, D♯, E, D♯, C♯, B, A, G♯, F♯, E.
Relative. 1, 2, 3, 4, 5, 6, 7, 8, 7, 6, 5, 4, 3, 2, 1.

Absolute. E, F♯, G♯, A, B, C♯, D♯, E, D♯, C♯, B, A, G♯, F♯, E.
Relative. 1, 2, 3, 4, 5, 6, 7, 8, 7, 6, 5, 4, 3, 2, 1.

224. Name pitches, absolute and relative.

do, do, re, mi, mi, fa, la, la, fa, fa, mi, mi, re,
Key-tone, re, three and four, Just the same as those be-fore,

do, do, re, mi, mi, fa, sol, la, sol, fa, mi, re, do.
Just as free, this you see, As in a-ny oth-er key.

225.

do, si, la, sol, sol, la, si, do, mi, re, do, mi, re, do,
Smooth-ly a-long, Glid-eth our song, Firm in the movement, Now

fa, mi, re, mi, mi, re, do, mi, re, do, sol, la, si, do.
stead-y and strong, True to the pitch-es, All right and none wrong

226. Question in regard to measure and pitches.

Do, re, mi, fa, sol, fa, mi, fa, mi, re, do, si, la, sol,

do, do, mi, sol, fa, mi, re, do.

227.

do mi, sol, fa, mi, re, do, si, do,   sol, mi, re,

do, mi, sol, fa, mi, re, do, si, do,   sol, sol, do.

228.

do, re, mi, re, mi, fa, mi, fa, sol, fa, sol, la, sol, fa, mi,

re,   sol,   do, sol, mi, do,   sol, do.

229.

do,   sol, mi, fa,   do,

fa,   sol,   do,   do,   fa,   sol,   do.

230. Compound double measure.

mi, mi, re, mi, sol, fa, re, re, do, re, mi, do, mi,   sol, fa,

re,   sol, la, si, do, sol,   mi, re, do. re, do.

All the World is Dazzling Snow.

Each part, then both parts.

Moderato.

do, do, mi, mi, sol, sol, mi, re, re, do, do, fa, mi, re,
1. All   the world is   daz-zling snow, Come, oh, come, and let us go
2. Thro' the shad-'wy woods we sweep, Up and down each shining steep;

do, do, do, do, sol. sol, do. sol, sol, la, la, si, do, sol,

All the World. Concluded.

do, do, mi, mi, sol, sol, mi, re, do, fa, mi, re, re, do.
Thro' the snow drifts, deep and white, Sparkling, changing, glitt'ring, bright.
O'er the froz - en brooks we glide, And where danc-ing shad-ows hide.

do, do, do, do, sol, sol, do, sol, la, si, do, sol, sol, do.

When is a Door? (Round in three parts.)

Moderato.

When is a door not a door? Give it up? When is a

door not a door? Let me see; Ah, yes, when it is a - jar.

Tick and Strike.

Sopranos.

In the farmer's kitch-en bright, The old clock ticks precise and clear,

Altos.

Al - ways right, al - ways right, Ev - 'ry day and ev - 'ry year.

Sopranos.

"Tick and strike!" "tick and strike!" That is what it seems to say,

Altos.

While the sea - sons come and go, And sun - ny locks turn gray.

CHORUS. *Sing prelude again before singing second verse.*

1. "Tick and strike!" "tick and strike!" That is what it seems to say,
2. Al - ways right, al - ways right, Ev - 'ry day and ev - 'ry year,

While the sea - sons come and go, And sun - ny locks turn gray.
In the farm - er's kitch - en bright, it ticks pre - cise and clear.

Morning Comes.

1. Morn-ing comes! morning comes! Trembling up the rip-pling tide;
2. Morn-ing comes! morning comes! Like a war-rior-an-gel sped;
3. Morn-ing comes! morning comes! Mail'd in gold and fire he stands.

Morn-ing comes! morn-ing comes! Spreading glo-ries far and wide.
Morn-ing comes! morn-ing comes! Light and life a-bout him shed.
Morn-ing comes! morn-ing comes! Wak-ing all the seas and lands.

Why Should a Sigh.

pAndantino.

1. Why should a sigh es-cape us, When parting hours do chime;
2. The dear-est friends must sever, Tho' keen may be the dart

We do not part for-ev-er; 'Tis on-ly for a time.
That parting leaves to rank-le In ev-'ry lov-ing heart;

Tho' far a-way I wan-der, Up-on the dark blue sea,
But lov'd one, till my com-ing, Faithful I'll keep to thee;

In song thine im-age ev-er Shall pres-ent be to me.
And in my song thine im-age Shall pres-ent be to me.

Always a Welcome.

Moderato.

1. Come in thy glad-ness, come in thy sor-row, Come when the
2. Come when life's troubles 'round thee are clinging, Come when thy
3. Come at thy pleasure, sure i' the greeting —On-ly de-

Always a Welcome. Concluded.

winds sweep o - ver the sea ; Come in the evening, come on the
heart filled with anguish may be ; Come when the spring-birds sweetly are
light our loved one shall see ; Whate'er the time or place of the

mor-row, Come! there is al - ways a wel-come for thee.
sing-ing, Come! there is al - ways a wel-come for thee.
meet-ing, Here there is al - ways a wel-come for thee.

KEY OF F.

231. After singing until the key of C is in mind drop B and substitute B-flat, and F will be found to be key-tone.

232. Sing the following lesson, beginning in the key of C

C, D, E, F, G, A, B, C, C, C, C, B-flat, A, G, F
do, re, mi, fa, sol, la, si, do, sol, sol, sol, fa, mi, re, do,

F, E, D, C, B-flat, A, B-flat, C, D, E, F, G, F.
do, si, la, sol, fa, mi, fa, sol, la, si, do, re, do.

233. It will be found that for representing this key all the degrees of the staff must be kept natural but one; that must be flatted.

234. Pitches of the key of F in scale form.

Absolute. F, G, A, B♭, C, D, E, F, E, D, C, B♭, A, G, F.
Relative. 1, 2, 3, 4, 5, 6, 7, 8, 7, 6, 5, 4, 3, 2, 1.

Absolute. F, G, A, B♭, C, D, E, F, E, D, C, B♭, A, G, F.
Relative. 1, 2, 3, 4, 5, 6, 7, 8, 7, 6, 5, 4, 3, 2, 1.

235.

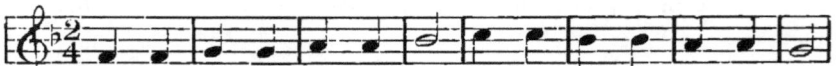

do, do, re, re, mi, mi, fa, sol, sol, fa, fa, mi, mi, re,
Tones re - lat - ed al-ways go Just the same from high to low,

do, do, re, re, mi, mi, fa, sol, sol, fa, fa, mi, re, do.
Where-so - e'er the pitch may be, What-so - ev - er be the key.

236.

do, si, la, sol, sol, la, si, do, re, do, si, la, sol, fa,
This is the work We will not shirk, Learning to read in this

mi, fa, sol, la, si, do, re, mi, re, do, re, do, si, do.
new key of F, Both in the treb-le and in the base clef.

237.

Do, re, mi, fa, sol, fa, mi, re, do, mi, sol, mi, re do, re,

do, do, mi, sol, fa, mi, re, do.

238.

Do, si, do, re, mi, re, do, si, la, si, do, re, do, si,

do, si, do, la, re, do, si, do, sol, do.

239.

Do, mi, do, sol, fa, mi, re, mi, do, sol, la, si, do,

sol, mi, do, fa, re, mi, fa, mi, sol, mi, do, fa, re, mi, re, do.

240.

Do, sol, mi, re, mi, fa, sol, la, la, sol, fa, mi, re, do,

mi, re, do, si, do, sol, do, mi

241.

Do,re,mi,do,   re, sol,   re,mi,fa, re,   mi,   do,   do,   re, la,

si,do,re, si,   do,   sol,fa,mi, sol,   sol,   sol,la,si, sol,   do.

Why Don't I Love You?

Moderato.

sol, do, do, do, do, mi, re, do, mi, sol, sol, sol, fa,   mi,   re,

1. Why don't I love you? I don't know! Love never gives a   rea - son;
2. Now list! and let me tell you this, And learn a lit - tle pru-dence;

sol, do, do, do, do, sol, sol, do, do, mi, mi, mi, re, do, sol,

sol, la, si, do, re, mi, do, fa, fa, sol, sol, fa, mi, re, do.
But that he has one I don't doubt---You do! that's downright treason.
'Tis not love's cus-tom to explain The wherefores to his stu-dents.

sol, fa, sol, la, si, do, do, fa, fa, mi, mi, re, do, sol, do.

What Financial Troubles?   (Round in Four Parts.)

Allegretto.

What fi - nan - cial troubles have the birds on sum-mer morn-ings?

Poor things! their lit - tle bills are all   o - ver dew (due).

Distant Bells.

Sopranos.

Dis-tant bells, dis-tant bells, Many a heart with sadness swells,

Altos.

While your soft and tender chiming Opes the door where mem'ry dwells.

Sopranos.

Hark! up-on the winds increasing, Now they come more loud and clear;

Altos.

Swinging, ringing, sighing, dy-ing, Now they fade up-on the ear.

CHORUS. Sing prelude again for second verse.

1. Dis-tant bells, dis-tant bells, Many a heart with sad-ness swells,
2. Dis-tant bells, dis-tant bells, Now they come more loud and clear,

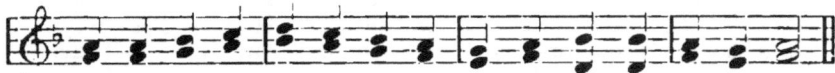

While your soft and tender chiming Opes the door where mem'ry dwells.
Swinging, ringing, sighing, dy-ing, Now they fade up-on the ear.

Echo, Echo, Every-where.

These duets are especially useful for practicing syllables, because no syllables are here printed.

Moderato.

1. Ech-o, ech-o, ev-'ry-where, Floating thro' the crys-tal air,
2. Ech-o, ech-o, ev-'ry-where, Floating thro' the crys-tal air,
3. Ech-o, ech-o, ev-'ry-where, Floating thro' the crys-tal air,
4. Ech-o answer now once more, Is it on the unknown shore?

f   *pp* **Echo.**

Where do liv-ing wa-ters flow? Do you know? No!
Where do fade-less flow-ers grow? Do you know? No!
Where are nev-er sounds of woe? Do you know? No!
Once a-gain the truth de-clare, Here or there? There!

Star of the Summer Night.

1. Star of the summer eve, Sink, sink to rest! Sink ere the sil - ver light
2. Wind of the summer eve, Waft, waft your sighs From where the distant hills
3. Bird of the summer eve, Chant, chant your song! While thro' the twilight gleams

Fades from the west, Sink ere the sil - ver light Fades from the west.
Kiss gold - en skies, From where the dis - tant hills Kiss gold - en skies.
Night's starry throng, While thro' the twilight gleams Night's starry throng.

Far, Far Away.

Melody in the alto. Cres., 1st and 3d lines; dim., 2d and 4th lines of each verse.

1. Friends and old com - pan-ions dear, Tho' far, far a - way,
2. Think not we can e'er for - get, Tho' far, far a - way,
3. Time steals on, and you re - main Still far, far a - way,

In our dreams you oft ap - pear, Tho' far, far a - way.
Those sweet hours when first we met, Tho' far, far a - way.
But we hope to meet a - gain, Tho' far, far a - way.

Come to the Meadow. (Vocal Waltz.)

Sometimes when it is desirable that the music should *look* fast, the eighth is used for beat-note. It would, however, go just as fast if the quarter were beat-note. The movement mark, and not the beat-note, decides the speed. Introduce sixteenths, first and second endings, etc.

1. Oh, come to the meadow where blossoms are springing, And
come, dear compan-ions, and join in their numbers, For
2. All beam-ing so bright-ly the brook-let is danc-ing, And
then, dear compan-ions, and join in its mu - sic, And

Come to the Meadow. Concluded.

sweet tones are float-ing far down in the val - ley, Oh,
beau - ty is round us this bright sum-mer [OMIT.] . . day.
sport - ive - ly kiss -ing the sweet mod- est flow - ers, Come,
cull from its beau - ties, this bright sum-mer [OMIT.] . . day.

Tra, la, la, la, la, la, la, la, la, la, la, la, la, la, la,

la, la, la, la, la, la, la, la, la, la, la, la, la, la, la, la, la.

KEY OF B FLAT.

242. From the tones of the key of F omit E and substitute E flat, and the key of B flat will be the result—that is, the tones will cluster around B flat as their "home," or key-tone.

243. Sing the following lesson, beginning in the key of F.

F, G, A, G, F, E, F, F, F, F, F, E flat,
do, re, mi, re, do, si, do, do, sol, sol, sol, fa,

D, E flat, F, F, F, G, F, E flat, D, C, B flat.
mi, fa, sol, sol, sol, la, sol, fa, mi, re, do.

244. Arrange the staff so that all pitches of the key will be represented. The arrangement will serve for "sign of key," or "signature."

245. The pitches of this key in scale form.

Absolute. B♭, C, D, E♭, F, G, A, B♭, A, G, F, E♭, D, C, B♭.
Relative. 1, 2, 3, 4, 5, 6, 7, 8, 7, 6, 5, 4, 3, 2, 1.

Absolute. B♭, C, D, E♭, F, G, A, B♭, A, G, F, E♭, D, C, B♭.
Relative. 1, 2, 3, 4, 5, 6, 7, 8, 7, 6, 5, 4, 3, 2, 1.

246.

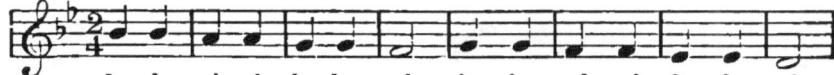

do, do, si, si, la, la, sol, la, la, sol, sol, fa, fa, mi,
See how firm this five can be, Then go on to plaintive three,

re, mi, fa, sol, la, si, do, re, re, do, do, si, si, do.
But for rest, when all is done, None is like the key-tone, one.

247.

do, re, mi, fa, mi, fa, sol, la, sol, la, si, do, si, la,
Ev-'ry new key makes us more free, Plac-ing the syl-la-bles

sol, fa, mi, re, do, re, mi, fa, sol, la, sol, la, si, do.
where they be-long, Making found-a-tions both sol-id and strong.

248. Moderato.

Do,   re,

do, mi, sol, do,   mi, re, do, si, la, si, do.

249. Boldly.

Sol, do,   sol, re,   sol, mi, re, do, si, do, si, la, sol,

do,   re,   mi,   la, si, do.

250. Gracefully.

Sol, do, do, si, sol, sol, sol, re, re, do, sol, sol, sol, mi, mi, mi, re, do,

si, la, si, do,   re, mi, fa, mi, re, do, re, do, si, do.

251. Moderato.

Do,   re,   do,   mi,

sol, fa, mi, fa, sol,   do,   mi,   sol, fa, mi, fa, sol,   do.

252. Compound double measure.

Do, re, do, si,   re, mi, re, do,   sol,   do,   fa, mi, re, mi,

fa, mi, fa, re,   mi, re, mi, do,   la, si, do, re, mi, fa, mi, re, do.

Down the Stream.

Andantino.

do, do, si, la, sol, fa, mi, fa, sol, la, si, do, re, si,
1. Down the stream of life we glide, On-ward, on-ward, side by side;
2. Ma - tin songs in ear - lier years, La - ter songs with sighs and tears;

do, do, do, do, do, do, do, re, mi, fa, sol, la, fa, sol,

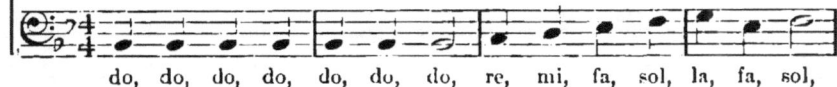

do, do, si, la, sol, fa, mi, fa, sol, la, re, do, si, do.
Drift-ing, ev - er drift - ing on, To the dist-ant shore be-yond.
Drift-ing on, thro' good and ill, To the har - bor calm and still.

do, do, do, do, do, do, do, re, mi, fa, fa, sol, sol, do.

Why is Athens?   (Round in Three Parts.)

Moderato.

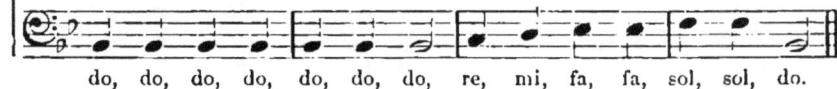

Why is Athens like the wick of a can - dle? You don't like to say,

But you must o - bey. Well, then, 'cause it's in the midst of Greece.

'Tis May.

Sopranos.

'Tis May, bright May, the merry air Is full of per-fume sweet;

'Tis May. Concluded.

On shrub and tree, 'mid springing grass, The new-born flow-ers meet.

The birds are in the wild-est joy, The blue sky smiles a-bove;

The mountain dons its em-'rald robe, And ver-dure decks the grove.

1. 'Tis May, bright May, the mer-ry air Is full of per-fume sweet;
2. 'Tis May, the birds are full of joy, The blue sky smiles a-bove;

On shrub and tree, 'mid springing grass, The new-born flow-ers meet.
The mountain dons its em-'rald robe, And ver-dure decks the grove.

God is Love.

1. God is love! the an-gels whisper, Hark! the ech-o in the air,
2. God is love! to you he call-eth, Sadden'd heart and troubled brow,

God is love! 'tis waft-ed ev-er O'er and o'er the world so fair.
God is love! oh, wea-ry mor-tal, Cast thy sor-row on him now.

Mother's Anchor.

1. Her anchor is a gold-en one, All wreathed about with ros-es,
2. How proudly rides the lit-tle craft Up-on life's peaceful wa-ters,
3. Oh, there, within her qui-et nook, Far, far from noise and ran-cor,

And in a sea of love and rest It grace-ful-ly re-pos-es.
For there the trip-le anch-or rests, In husband, sons and daught-ers.
She holds with confi-dence and trust To her be-lov-ed anch-or.

Summer Morn.

1. Oh, I love thy dews so pearl-y, sum-mer morn, summer morn;
2. Oh, I love thy song of la-bor, sum-mer morn, summer morn;
3. Yes, I love thy dews so pearl-y, sum-mer morn, summer morn:

And thy first cool hours so ear-ly, sum-mer morn, sum-mer morn;
From the thrift-y bus-y neigh-bor, sum-mer morn, sum-mer morn;
And thy first cool hours so ear-ly, sum-mer morn, sum-mer morn;

For the freshest tho'ts are giv-en When the eastern bars are riv-en,
While he seeks with joy and pleasure For the deep-ly hid-den treasure
For the freshest tho'ts are giv-en When the eastern bars are riv-en,

And the new light comes from heaven, sum-mer morn, sum-mer morn.
Which thou givest with-out meas-ure, sum-mer morn, sum-mer morn.
And the new light comes from heaven, sum-mer morn, sum-mer morn.

KEY OF E-FLAT.

253. From the key of B-flat, omit A and substitute A-flat, and the key of E-flat will be the result.

254. Sing the following lesson, beginning in the key of B-flat and ending in the new key. Begin with the upper B-flat.

B♭, A, G, A, B♭, B♭, B♭, B♭, B♭, A♭, G, F, E♭, F, G, A♭, B♭, A♭, G, F, E♭, D, E♭.
do, si, la, si, do, sol, sol, sol, sol, fa, mi, re, do, re, mi, fa, sol, fa, mi, re, do, si, do.

255. Make the staff represent this key, and the peculiar arrangement will become the signature or sign of the key.

256. Tones of the key of E-flat in scale form.

Absolute. E♭, F, G, A♭, B♭, C, D, E♭, D, C, B♭, A♭, G, F, E♭.
Relative. 1, 2, 3, 4, 5, 6, 7, 8, 7, 6, 5, 4, 3, 2, 1.

Absolute. E♭, F, G, A♭, B♭, C, D, E♭, D, C, B♭, A♭, G, F, E♭.
Relative. 1, 2, 3, 4, 5, 6, 7, 8, 7, 6, 5, 4, 3, 2, 1.

257.

do, re, mi, mi, re, mi, fa, mi, fa, sol, sol, fa, sol, la,
Ei-ther we have been re - miss, Or we've had a key like this.

la, la, sol, sol, fa, fa, mi, la, la, sol, fa, mi, re, do.
No, there's much twixt this and that, That was E and this E-flat.

258.

do, sol, do, re, re, sol, re, mi, mi, sol, mi, fa, sol, fa,
There is no E here in this key, Tho' as we're sing-ing the

mi, re, do, re, re, sol, re, mi, sol, mi, fa, mi, re, do.
syl-la-bles o'er They're on the self-same de-grees as be-fore.

259. Having practiced in the key of E, which *looks* like this, it will not be necessary to indicate syllables fully here.

Do,   sol, fa, mi, fa, sol, do, sol,

do,   re,

260.

Do, re, mi, sol, do,   fa, mi, re, do, si, la, sol, do, re, mi, sol,

la, fa, re,   la, fa, re,   do, mi, sol, sol, do.

261.

Do, re, mi, sol, fa, mi, re, sol, do,   do, mi, sol, do.

si, la, sol, mi, do,   sol, fa, re, do, do, sol, mi, do, fa, re, do.

262.

Sol, fa, mi, re, mi, fa, mi, do, mi, re, do, si, do, re, do, re, mi, fa, re,

mi, sol, re, re, mi, sol, mi, do, mi, re, do, si, do, re, do.

Our Princess.

Allegretto.

1. She lives with-in a qui-et home, No mod-el of the grac-es,
2. From morn till eve our lit-tle girl Is bus-y at her la-bor;
3. Long may she bravely smile on us, Our dar-ling household fair-y,

Un-known to cul-ture's high-er walks Or fashion's gid-dy plac-es.
She sweeps and dusts the old farmhouse, Or help a poor-er neighbor.
The queen of gar-den, house and lot, And princess of the dai-ry.

When is a Man? (Round in three parts.)

When is a man not a man? tell me that! *Is it when he's sow-ing!*

Is it that! Pshaw! no, it is when he's a Shav-ing.

The Rainy Day.

Sopranos.

Oh, there is no sound in nature, When the sun has parch'd the plain,

Altos.

Like the beat-ing on the shingles Of the gen-tle sum-mer rain;

The Rainy Day. Concluded.

Sopranos.

And we love to list-en to it, Rest-ing on the fra-grant hay:

Altos.

That is so, there's noth-ing like A good old-fash-ioned rain-y day.

CHORUS. Prelude twice.

1. Ha! ha! ha! there's nothing sweeter, When the sun has parch'd the plain,
2. It recalls the sounds of childhood, When all e - vil kept a - loof;

Than the beat-ing on the shin-gles Of the gen-tle sum-mer rain.
Noth-ing wakes a sweet-er mem-'ry Than the rain-drops on the roof.

Morning Echoes.

Moderato.

1. Hear the morning ech-oes ring-ing From the hill-y slope so fair;
2. Yes, the hills send back their greeting In the shepherds' glad re-frain;
3. Sweetest tones the vales are fill-ing, As the sing-ers move a-long,

How they answer back the sing-ing Of the shepherds gathered there.
Then a-gain the tones re-peat-ing, They prolong the hap-py strain.
Ev-'ry peak re-spons-ive thrill-ing To their joyous morning song.

Refrain.

'Tis ech-o an-swers there, In the morn-ing air,

Ech-o, ech-o, ech-o, ech-o, ech-o, ech-o, In the morning air.

The Blacksmith. (Round in four parts.)

Now the blacksmith's arm is swinging, And his cheerful

song he's sing-ing, Kling! kling! Klang! klang!

Starry Waves.

Coming on last half of beat.   Practice thoroughly with syllables.

1. Star - ry waves, star - ry waves, Danc-ing   on   the   sea,
2. Earth and air, earth and   air, With bright fair - ies teem,

Bright-ly come, dark-ly fade, Die   in   mel - o - dy; The
From the moon glid-ing down On   each   sil - ver beam; The

moonbeams gen - tly fall Up - on   the dreaming flow'rs, On
wav - ing flow - er - bells Hold many an el - fin sprite, And

fra - grant for - est trees, And bloom-ing myr - tle bow'rs.
fair - y   mu - sic floats Up - on   the   si - lent night.

Westward.

Moderato.

1. Far, far I'm go-ing to the land I love best,   O - ver the
2. Far, far I'm go-ing, but will some day re - turn, Where bright the

mountains to the bright golden west; There, there I'll work and wait for
fires   of the old homestead burn; Then in the brightness of our

days that will come, There will I make for all my loved ones a home.
hope's ardent glow, Out to our western home to-geth - er we'll go.

KEY OF A-FLAT.

263. From the key of E flat omit D and substitute D flat, and the key of A flat will be the result.

264. The following lesson begins in E flat, but soon goes into the key of A flat by substituting D flat for D.

E♮, F, G, A♮, B♮, A♮, G, F, E♮, E♮, E♮, E♮, E♮, D♮, C, B♮, A♮, B♮, C, D♮,
do, re, mi, fa, sol, fa, mi, re, do, sol, sol, sol, sol, fa, mi, re, do, re, mi, fa,

　　　E♮, F, G, A♮, B♮, C, D♮, E♮, A♮, G, F, G, A♮.
　　　sol, la, si, do, re, mi, fa, sol, do, si, la, si, do.

265. Make lines and spaces represent correctly the pitches of this key, and that arrangement will become the signature to the key, shortened for common use to "four flats."

266. Pitches of this key in scale form.

Absolute.	A♮,	B♮,	C,	D♮,	E♮,	F,	G,	A♮,	G,	F,	E♮,	D♮,	C,	B♮,	A♮.
Relative.	1,	2,	3,	4,	5,	6,	7,	8,	7,	6,	5,	4,	3,	2,	1.

Absolute.	A♮,	B♮,	C,	D♮,	E♮	F,	G,	A♮,	G,	F,	E♮,	D♮,	C,	B♮,	A♮.
Relative.	1,	2,	3,	4,	5,	6,	7,	8,	7,	6,	5,	4,	3,	2,	1.

267.

do, do, re, re, mi, re, do,　si, si, do, do, si, la, sol,
Each degree has now been "do," Twice, this one, as we all know;

do, do, re, re, mi, re, do,　sol, sol, la, la, si, si, do.
C, G, D, A, E, don't miss! F, B flat, E flat, and this.

268.

do, re, mi, fa, mi, re, do, sol, do, si, la, sol, mi, do,
Now we proclaim, Keys are the same, In their re - la - tion and

re, mi, fa, mi, do, re, do, si, la, sol, fa, mi, re, do.
rel - a - tive name; If we don't know that, we're all much to blame.

269.

Do, si, do, sol, la, si, do, re,

do, si, do, sol, la,　　　do, mi, re, do.

270.

Do, sol, mi, sol, do, mi, re, do, si, la, sol,

la, do, si, do, mi, do, sol, mi, la, do, si, do.

271.

Mi, re, do, si, si, la, fa, sol,

do, si, la, re, do, si, do, re, mi, sol, la, re,

272.

273.

From the Tower.

Andante.

do, si, do,

1. From the tow'r, Hark, the bell Tolls the old year's pass-ing knell!
2. Time brings change, Joys and cares, Stealing on us un - a - wares;

do, re, mi,

Ah! how swift the months have fled Since the last old year lay dead!
Be the New Year swift or long, Love is liv - ing, faith is strong.

The Yankee Boy. (Round in three parts.)

The Yan-kee boy his draft has cash'd, His thanks he's just re-

turn-ing; Why is he like the par-lor grate That is well fill'd and

burn-ing? Think it o-ver well, it will take a lit-tle craft, —

He is *all-fir-ed grate-ful* on ac-count of the *draft.*

The Sunbeams.

Andante.

1. The sunbeams gild the val-ley With mild and gen-tle ray;
2. The birds are warbling glad-ly In din-gle and in dell,
3. Their light and joy and gladness Il-lu-mine all the scene;

All na-ture bliss-ful smil-ing Now hails the king of day.
While beauteous golden sunbeams Weave round their mag-ic spell.
They lin-ger on the o-cean, They clothe the hills with green

Chestnuts.

ORENA LEE.
Moderato.   ✻

1. The chest-nuts were ripe in the val-ley be-low— A
2. "Let's go and camp out the whole day in the woods!" 'Twas
3. The moments swift glide, while so gay-ly we ride, And
4. Such heaps of rich treas-ures we gath-ered that day, The

Mister John Frost told the sto-ry; The sky was so blue, and the
car-ried by loud ac-cla-ma-tions. Old Gray nev-er drew such a
soon in the val-ley we're searching; For chest-nut groves hide where the
squirrels, I fear, will re-mem-ber; Then rest-ed and lunched, and grew

Chestnuts. Concluded.

Oc to - ber glow Crown'd for - est and hill - top with glo - ry.
queer load of goods, Nor sol - dier such boun - ti - ful ra - tions.
squir - rels a - bide, Red rogues 'mong the thick branches perch - ing.
hap - py and gay O'er feasts in the com - ing De - cem - ber.

274. The following lessons are for the practice of sixteenth notes, and of the dotted quarter followed by the eighth, and for the dotted eighth followed by the sixteenth, and for other rhythmic forms.

Let Us See.

Moderato.

Let us see, see if we a - gree, Let us see if we can all a-

gree To sing this song of mer - ry glee, Let us see if we a-

gree, Yes, let us see if we a - gree, yes, see if we a - gree.

Now, Kind Friends.

Think of *all* the words of the first measure while singing the third and fifth measures; also all the words of the ninth measure while singing the eleventh and thirteenth measures. This is to help in acquiring the ability to sing dotted quarters followed by eighths, while beating time.

Now, kind friends, to all, Now, friends, to all, Now to all we say "good night;"

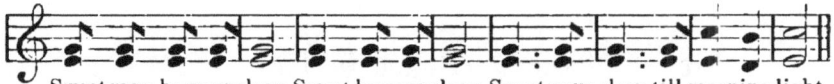

Sweet may be your sleep, Sweet be your sleep, Sweet your sleep till morning light.

Oh, Come, Come Away.

Allegretto.   German.

1. Oh, come, come a - way, from la - bor now re - pos - ing, Let
2. From toil and the cares on which the day is clos - ing, The
3. The bright day is gone, the moon and stars ap - pear - ing, With

Oh, Come, Come Away. Concluded.

bus - y care a - while for-bear, Oh, come, come a - way! Oh,
hour of eve brings sweet reprieve, Oh, come, come a - way! In
sil - ver light il - lume the night, Oh, come, come a - way! We'll

come, our so - cial joys re - new, And here, where trust and
tones of love and sym - pa - thy, We'll sing in tune - ful
join in grate - ful songs of praise To him who crowns our

friendship grew, Let true hearts welcome you; Oh, come, come a-way!
har - mo - ny, Of hope, joy, lib - er - ty; Oh, come, come a-way!
peace-ful days With health, hope, happiness; Oh, come, come a-way!

Thirty Days. (Round in Six Parts.)

G. F. R.

Thir - ty days hath Sep-tem - ber, A - pril, June, and No-vem - ber,

All the rest have thir-ty - one, Sav-ing Feb-ru - a - ry a - lone,

Which has twenty-eight, rain or shine, And on leap-year twenty-nine.

Sing Together. (Round in Three Parts.)

Introduce *Triplet.*

Sing, sing to-geth-er, Mer-ri-ly, mer-ri-ly sing; Sing, sing to-

geth - er, Mer-ri-ly, mer-ri-ly sing, Sing, sing, sing, sing.

The Merry Skaters.

In the following songs one part may be sung,—or two parts, making a duet,—or adding the base, three parts, making a trio.

1. Oh, how the mer-ry peal rings out, Huz-za!   With
2. And see, they dart as if on wings, Huz-za!   In
3. Ah, joy-ful in our northern clime, Huz-za!   The

Huz-za!

many a laugh and many a shout, Huz-za!   With
lines and curves and spi-ral flings, Huz-za!   In
mer-ry shout and ring-ing chime, Huz-za!   The

Huz-za!

many a laugh and many a shout, O'er all the i-cy
lines and curves and spi-ral flings, While clear and bright the
mer-ry shout and ring-ing chime Of ska-ters in the

fields a-bout, Huz-za! huz-za! Huz-za! huz-za!
i-ron rings, Huz-za! huz-za! Huz-za! huz-za!
win-ter time, Huz-za! huz-za! Huz-za! huz-za!

Happily. (Compound Double Measure.)

When six eighths in a measure are to be sung somewhat fast, it is easier to group them into two groups of three eighths in each group, and give a down beat to the first group, and up beat for the second group. This makes what is called *Compound Double Measure.* As the dotted quarter is just equal to three eighths, the dotted quarter is beat-note. The second syllable of each of these words should have the same vowel sound that each last syllable has,—as if the words were spelled happy-ly, sleepy-ly, etc. Not the vowel sound of "u" in "thus." In two divisions. Let the first division get one measure the start, then sing "round and round," using the last measure only to end with.

Moderato.

Happi - ly, sleepi - ly, clumsi - ly, drowsi - ly, craft-i - ly, eas - i - ly,
Mer-ri - ly, handi - ly, sau-ci - ly, stin-gi - ly, guilt-i - ly, gloomi-ly,

To end with.

loft - i - ly, haughti - ly, dain - ti - ly, wit - ti - ly　sing.
flash-i - ly, la - zi - ly, ver - i - ly, bus - i - ly　sing.

Old Sayings.

MRS. M. A. KIDDER.　　　　　　　　　　　　　　　　　✱

This exercise is for rapid articulation. Let the first verse be sung *Moderato* (two beats in the measure), the second verse *Allegro,* and the third *Presto.* These movements may be ascertained by attaching a pocket knife or any light weight to a string and let it swing like a pendulum. Two feet of string will give the first movement, one foot will give the second, and six inches the third.

1. As poor as a church mouse, As thin as a rail, As fat as a
2. As pure as a lil - y, As neat as a pin, As smart as a
3. As clean as a pen - ny, As dark as a pall, As hard as a

por-poise, As rough as a gale, As brave as a li - on, As
steel-trap, As ug - ly as sin, As dead as a door-nail, As
mill-stone, As bit - ter as gall, As fine as a fid - dle, As

spry as a cat, As bright as a sixpence, As weak as a rat;
white as a sheet, As flat as a pan-cake, As red as a beet;
clear as a bell, As dry as a her-ring, As deep as a well;

Old Sayings. Concluded.

As proud as a pea-cock, As sly as a fox, As mad as a
As round as an ap - ple, As black as your hat, As brown as a
As light as a feath - er, As hard as a rock, As sharp as a

March hare, As strong as an ox, As fair as a lil - y, As
ber - ry, As blind as a bat, As mean as a mis - er, As
nee - dle, As calm as a clock, As green as a gos - ling, As

emp-ty as air, As rich as a Crœ-sus, As cross as a bear.
full as a tick, As plump as a partridge, As square as a brick.
brisk as a bee—And this is the end of The re - per - to - ry.

Happiness for Him who Will.

Allegretto.

1. Mer - ri - ly the sunbeams Shimmer o'er the meadow, Fit - ful - ly the
2. When the falling snowflakes Cov - er up the flow - ers, When the wa-ter
3. Hear the mer-ry chil-dren Laughing in the snow-drift, See the hard - y

wa - ter Sparkles in the rill; Cheeri - ly the bee hums 'Mid the summer
rip - ples In the ice are still; Then the lit-tle snow-bird Whistles on the
coast-ers Sliding down the hill; Ev' - ry one is joy - ful, All the world are

flow - ers, "Hap - pi - ness is ev - 'ry-where for him who will."
fence - rail, "Hap - pi - ness is ev - 'ry-where for him who will."
say - ing, "Hap - pi - ness is ev - 'ry-where for him who will."

Pray.

G. F. R.

Moderato.

1. Go, when the morn-ing shin-eth, Go, when the moon is bright,
2. Go with the pur-est feel-ing, Put earth-ly tho'ts a-way,

Go, when the eve de-clin-eth, Go in the hush of night.
And in His pres-ence kneel-ing, Do thou in se-cret pray.

Sing all the More.

✱

Allegretto.

1. If you have not sung at all, Now's the time for one and
2. Will you try it once a-gain? Will you try our mer-ry
3. Now a rous-ing cho-rus, all, Let it ring throughout the

all; If you say we've sung be-fore, Then we say sing all the
strain? Did you say "we sang be-fore?" Then we say sing all the
hall; Tho' you sang it well be-fore, Still we say sing all the

more, Then we say sing all the more, sing all the more.
more, Then we say sing all the more, sing all the more.
more, Still we say sing all the more, sing all the more.

God Speed the Right.

German.

Maestoso.

1. Now to heaven our prayer as-cend - ing, God speed the right;
2. Be that prayer a - gain re-peat - ed—God speed the right;
3. Pa - tient, firm and per - se - ver - ing; God speed the right;

In a no - ble cause con-tend - ing, God speed the right.
Ne'er de-spair -ing, tho' de - feat - ed, God speed the right.
Ne'er th'event nor dan - ger fear - ing, God speed the right.

Be our zeal in heaven re - cord - ed, With suc - cess on
Like the good and great in sto - ry, If we fail, we
Pains, nor toils, nor tri - als heed - ing, In the strength of

earth re - ward-ed, God speed the right, God speed the right.
fail with glo - ry, God speed the right, God speed the right.
heaven succeeding—God speed the right, God speed the right.

Boys Wanted.

Con spirito.

1. Boys of spir-it, boys of will, Boys of mus-cle, brain and pow'r,
2. Not the weak and whining drones, That all troub-le mag-ni-fy—
3. Do what-e'er you have to do, With a true and hon-est zeal;

Fit to cope with an-y-thing; These are want-ed ev-'ry hour.
Not the ones who say "I can't," But the ones who say "I'll try."
Bend your sin-ews to the task; Put your shoulders to the wheel.

REFRAIN.

Boys want-ed! boys want-ed! Boys of mus-cle, brain and pow'r;

Boys want-ed! boys want-ed! These are want-ed ev-'ry hour.

Farewell. (Round in Two Parts.)

1. Now we say fare-well, Our pleas-ant work is done; Good

2. bye, then, good bye, then, all, un-til to-mor-row's sun.

My Song.

G. F. R.

1. At my work I'm always sing - ing, Tho' the day be cold and long,
2. I am sing-ing of the sun-shine, Tho' the sky is dull and gray;
3. I am sing-ing of the gar - den— Of the ros - es there in bloom,—

For my heart's so full of mu - sic That I can not stop the song.
I am sing-ing of the flow - ers All the chil-ly win - ter day.
Of a thousand things in na - ture,'Mid the win-ter's sullen gloom.

I am singing, I'm singing, Tho' the days be cold and long,

I am sing-ing, yes, I'm singing, Tho' the days be cold, be cold and long.

For my heart's so full of mu - sic That I can not stop my song.

Three Things. (Round in Four Parts.)

1.
2.

Three things are sought for, pow'r, pleas-ure, and wealth;

3.
4.

One spoils our tem - per, and two spoil our health.

Our Song-Birds.

Orena Lee.

1. Snow-bird sweet! Snow-bird sweet! Gold-brown coat and little bare feet; Come, my
2. Rob-in red, Rob-in red! Gai-ly singing "winter has fled;" On the
3. Red-bird gay! Red-bird gay! Why so quickly glancing a - way? In the
4. Coo, dove, coo, Coo, dove, coo, Dear thy note so ten-der and true; In the

snow-bird sweet, come around my door, When the cold winds wail, and the
brown hill-side by the laughing rill, There I hear thee warbling thy
morn-ing glow, at the sun-set hour, Comes thy wings' bright gleam with a
crowd-ed street, in the home of love, There is naught more pure than the

REFRAIN.

snow storms roar.
sweet song still.   Hark! hark! Tra, la, la, la, la, Tra, la,
witch-ing power.
snow-white dove.

la, la, la, Tra, la, la, la, la, la, la, la, la, la, la.

Float Away.

1. Float a-way, float a-way, o'er the far roll-ing sea;
2. Ro-vers we, ro-vers we, That can brook no re-straint;
3. O'er the sea, o'er the sea, Yes, for-ev-er we'll roam,

Snow-y sails, snow-y sails on its bos-om are free;
All the land nar-row seems, All its air has a taint;
On its breast, on its breast We will e'er find a home;

With the a-zure vault a-bove, And the li-quid blue be-low,
So we leap up-on our deck, And we spread a-loft each sail,
Wheth-er zeph-yrs kiss the wave, Or the tem-pest rage a-bove,

Mid the glo-rious bil-lows swell-ing high, O'er the o-cean we go.
Till, far out up-on the foam-y tide, We de-light in the gale.
And the seeth-ing mountains round us rise, Still the o-cean we love.

They March to the Rolling Drum. (Round in three parts.)

They march, they march to the roll-ing drum, The

Roll the R.

sol-diers bold! see, they come, they come, to the r-r-r-r-oll-ing drum.

INTERVALS.

MAJOR AND MINOR SECONDS, AND STEPS AND HALF-STEPS.

NOTE TO TEACHER.—In the writer's opinion, it is not best to touch this subject until the class have sung at least once through the keys. It is not really *needed* until chromatic tones are to be introduced.

When the class are ready for the subject, however, this is one way to teach it: Teacher sings two tones (say C and G) and asks how many tones he sang, and then asks the class to do the same. The difference of pitch between two tones is called an interval. (He questions.) Listen again and tell me if the interval I now give is larger or smaller than the other. (He sings, say C and E.) After they answer correctly and sing the same, he gives them C and D, and they say it is smaller, and sing it. Then he sings C and D-flat, and they say that is still smaller, and they sing that. Then he says: You see there are intervals of various sizes, but we will, for the present, only study these two smaller ones. I'll give you again the larger of the two, and you give it after me. (They sing C and D.)

There are two names for every interval—one to describe the musical effect that the two tones produce, and the other to show how far apart the two tones are. The name for the musical effect is a *Major Second*. The name for the difference of pitch is a *Step*—that is, tones to produce a *major second* must be a *step* apart. He sings, and they sing after him, C and D-flat. He names the musical effect *Minor Second*, and says that tones to produce a minor second must be a *half-step* apart. He then drills for some time, giving major seconds and minor seconds with his voice or an instrument (the voice is best), they naming as they hear. Then he calls for major and minor seconds, and they practice them until they can sing them correctly.

Now, let us understand one thing clearly before going on. We *hear* major and minor seconds, but we do *not* hear steps and half-steps. They are merely things to measure with. I do not call for steps and half-steps, because I do not think you can sing steps and half-steps. You sing major and minor seconds. You use the terms steps and half-steps for calculating purposes.

The word interval, then, means two different things. In one way of regarding it, it is something to hear, and in the other it is nothing to hear, but a difference of pitch, or, as it were, a distance. This is true because major and minor seconds, major and minor thirds, perfect fourths, fifths, etc., the world over, are called intervals, as certainly as the difference of pitch *between* any two is called an interval.

Now, let us take the tones of a key, ascending in scale order from a key tone, and see what kind of interval each two will make. I may say that any two tones of a key that are next to each other in scale order, always make either a major or a minor second. They are always either a step or a half-step apart. Do you think you will be able to tell whether I sing a major or a minor second as I sing up the scale? (They think they will, but, if they have not tried it before, they probably will not—three and four will seem at first to be a major second.)

Teacher sings C and D; all sing the same. Which is that, a major second or a minor second? How far apart are the tones in a major second? He sings C and D-flat, but does not tell them what he sings. Was that a major second or minor second? They answer, minor second. How far were the tones apart? They answer, half-step. They sing same, and then come D and E, and D and E-flat, with similar work. Now I will sing E and F, three and four of this key, and all go by hearing rather than by previous knowledge. He sings, perhaps beginning back at C to get all the tones well in mind, and then asks, "Do E and F produce a major second or a minor second?" The answer will probably be, major second. How far apart are the pitches E and F, then? "A step," is the answer. Well, you may all begin at C, and sing slowly C, D, E, and then, instead of going up a step, go up a half-step. This they will find they can not do, and so will be easily led to see that from E to F is a half step, or that those two tones produce a minor second. Similar work with F, G; G, A; A, B, and B, C, will show the intervals that the tones of a key make when in scale form. It would be well to show that the same intervals in the same order are found in every other key. (We are only dealing with major keys as yet.) For explanation of the interval produced by C and C-sharp (which is *not* a minor second, although the two tones are a half-step apart), and for more full teaching on the subject, see "Normal Musical Hand-book," p. 190. The class are now ready for Chromatic tones.

DIATONIC AND CHROMATIC TONES (TONE PITCHES.)

275. The regular members of keys (one, two, three, four, five, six, seven, eight) are said to be *Diatonic tones.*

276. The Diatonic tones are the *natural sounding* tones (using the word natural with its common meaning and not with its musical technical meaning.)

277. In the key of C the Diatonic tones are C, D, E, F, G, A, and B. In the key of G, G, A, B, C, D, E and F-sharp are diatonic. In the key of D both F-sharp and C-sharp are diatonic; and so on.

278. During a piece of music tones may be introduced that do not belong to the key in which the piece begins. Such tones may be members of another key introduced temporarily. If so, they are still diatonic tones. (See Modulation.) But if they do not lead into another key, they are said to be *Chromatic tones.* Chromatic tones are not the natural sounding tones of music, although they are most agreeable visitors, producing variety and richness in melody and harmony.

279. F-sharp, which is diatonic in the keys of G, D, A, and several others, is chromatic in the key of C, because it is not a regular member there. C, which is diatonic in so many keys, is chromatic in the keys of D, A, E, etc.

B is diatonic in the keys of C, G, D, A, E, B and F-sharp, but it is chromatic in the keys of F, B-flat, E-flat, A-flat, etc. B-flat, which is diatonic in the keys just named, is chromatic in the key of C and many others.

280. Every tone-pitch in music may be made diatonic or chromatic by relationship.

281. Put the tones of any key into scale form, introducing an intermediate tone where it can be done, and the *chromatic scale* of that key will be the result.

282. In the descending chromatic scale the intermediate tones are named and represented differently from what they are in the ascending.

283. CHROMATIC SCALE—KEY OF C.

With Absolute Names, Relative Names, and Syllables.

C, C-sharp, D, D-sharp, E, F, F-sharp, G, G-sharp, A, A-sharp, B, C,
1, sharp 1, 2, sharp 2, 3, 4, sharp 4, 5, sharp 5, 6, sharp 6, 7, 8,
Do, di, re, ri, mi, fa, fi, sol, si, la, li, si, do,

C, B, B-flat, A, A-flat, G, G-flat, F, E, E-flat, D, D-flat, C.
8, 7, flat 7, 6, flat 6, 5, flat 5, 4, 3, flat 3, 2, flat 2, 1.
do, si, se, la, le, sol, se, fa, mi, me, re, ra, do.

284. CHROMATIC SCALE—KEY OF D.

D, D-sharp, E, E-sharp, F-sharp, G, G-sharp, A, A-sharp, B, B-sharp, C-sharp D,
1, sharp 1, 2, sharp 2, 3, 4, sharp 4, 5, sharp 5, 6, sharp 6, 7, 8,
do, di, re, ri, mi, fa, fi, sol, si, la, li, si, do,

D, C-sharp, C, B, B-flat, A, A-flat, G, F-sharp, F, E, E-flat, D.
8, 7, flat 7, 6, flat 6, 5, flat 5, 4, 3, flat 3, 2, flat 2, 1.
do, si, se, la, le, soi, se, fa, mi, me, re, ra, do.

285. CHROMATIC SCALE—KEY OF B-FLAT.

B-flat, B, C, C-sharp, D, E-flat, E, F, F-sharp, G, G-sharp, A, B-flat,
1, sharp 1, 2, sharp 2, 3, 4, sharp 4, 5, sharp 5, 6, sharp 6, 7, 8,
do, di, re, ri, mi, fa, fi, sol, si, la, li, si, do,

B-flat, A, A-flat, G, G-flat, F, F-flat, E-flat, D, D-flat, C, C-flat, B-flat.
8, 7, flat 7, 6, flat 6, 5, flat 6, 4, 3, flat 3, 2, flat 2, 1.
do, si, se, la, le, sol, se, fa, mi, me, re, ra, do.

NOTE.—Observe that the natural acts sometimes like a flat and sometimes like a sharp. Flat seven and flat three in the key of D are indicated by means of a natural, and sharp one and sharp four in the key of B-flat are indicated by the same sign. Always think of *pitch* in connection with a "natural," and never of *naturalness*.

286. The syllables that are used for chromatic tones are spelled and pronounced, as the diatonic syllables are, according to the Italian mode.

287. The names one, two, three, four, five, six, seven and eight, are diatonic names; the others are, strictly speaking, chromatic names (sharp one, flat seven, etc.)

288. The syllables do, re, mi, fa, sol, la, si, do, are diatonic syllables; the others are, strictly speaking, chromatic syllables. The words "strictly speaking" are here used because sometimes, in short modulations, both chromatic names and chromatic syllables are applied to diatonic tones.

MODULATION.

289. A pleasant effect is often produced by going temporarily to another **key** during the course of a piece of music. This is called *modulating*, and the phrase or section from another key so introduced is called a *modulation*.

290. Modulations are not represented in the signature-place, but in the measures where they occur.

291. To make a sharped degree of the staff stand for the next lower pitch, a character called a "natural" is put upon it. To make a flatted degree of the staff stand for the next higher pitch, the same character (natural) is used; so the natural acts sometimes like a flat and sometimes like a sharp.

292. Sharps, flats, and naturals, when elsewhere than in the signature-place, are called *Accidentals*. The effect of an accidental continues only through the remainder of the measure in which it occurs, and is confined to the degree on which it is placed—does not effect the octaves above and below, as the same character would in the signature-place.

293. Syllables may be applied in a modulation as belonging to the key introduced, or they may be applied to the foreign tones as if they were chromatic tones. (See example of both ways in "Universal Praise," p. 84. It should, however, be remembered that the F-sharps in this piece, and the foreign tones generally in modulations, are not chromatic tones, but are diatonic in the keys introduced, and it is often an advantage to a class to name pitches and apply syllables accordingly.) A good rule is this: When the modulation is short do not change naming or syllables, but treat the new tones as chromatic; but when the modulation occupies a line or a section, then change relative naming and syllables to the key introduced.

294. It is a mistaken idea that accidentals always help to represent chromatic tones. They more commonly help to represent the diatonic tones of other keys in modulations.

295. To discover whether foreign tones in a piece of music are chromatic tones or diatonic tones of some other key, listen for key-tone. If key-tone does not change in your mind, the strange tones are chromatic. If the key-tone does change, they are diatonic, and a modulation has taken place. In the round, Glory Hallelujah, page 83, there is the feeling that C is home, or key-tone, all the way through; therefore, the F-sharps and D-sharps there introduced are chromatic tones, pleasantly *coloring* the music, but not changing key-tone.

MINOR KEYS.

296. The keys we have been using are called *Major keys*.

297. From any major key drop out five and substitute sharp five, and the relative *Minor key* of that major key will be the result. The sharp five will become seven of the new key. For instance, sing the following phrase in one of our major keys and add the key-tone which is here omitted:

do,   do,   si,   si,   la,   la,   sol,   la,   do,   si,   la,   sol, sol.
Firm the num - bers roll   a - long   Of this cheer-ful ma - jor-

When you give the key-tone to end with, supply a good word to rhyme with the last syllable of "along."

298. Now take the same tone pitches, only drop out five and substitute a pitch a half-step higher. You will find that will change the whole character of these tones. It will make them all more plaintive, and not only give a new key-tone but a new kind of key.

Supply key-tone, right syllable, and a good word to end with.

do, do, si, si, la, la, si, la, do, si, la, si, si,
Sad the strain to you and me, Of this plaintive mi - nor—

299. Every major key has its relative minor, that may be made from it in this way. A major and a minor key so related have the same signature, the tone that is peculiar to the minor key being always represented by the aid of an accidental.

300. One and two of any minor key are a step apart, and produce, when heard, a major second. Two and three are a half-step apart, and produce a minor second. Three and four are a step apart, and produce a major second. Four and five, same. Five and six, half-step,—minor second. Six and seven make an augmented second, and are a step-and-a-half apart (an interval that is not in major keys); and seven and eight, half-step,—minor second.

SYNCOPATION AND OTHER IRREGULAR ACCENTUATION.

301. Regular or Natural accent is when the accent in our singing exactly coincides with the accented beats in our minds. For instance (let the class all sing this):

Come to the fields, Oh, come, come, come! Oh,

come let us go! Oh, come, let us go!

302. When a tone commences on an unaccented beat and continues through an accented one, it is said to be a *syncopated tone.* The syncopated tone has usually to be accented, to produce a conflict with the regular accent of the measure. Here is an example (let the class all sing this):

We will not go, no! no! no! We

will not go, no! We will not go, no!

Strike the syncopated tones hard. Let there be a conflict between them and the regular accent that is in your own mind, Beat the time,—that is important. When this is well done, divide the class in two sections and sing those two numbers together. This will give an idea of the practical effect of the most common kind of syncopation.

303. Another kind of syncopation is made by commencing a tone on the last half of one beat, and continuing it through the first half of the next one. Beat the time and sing the following examples, first separately, then together—in two sections.

First.

The sunbeams are glancing, the brooklets are danc-ing, All na-ture is robed in bri-dal ar - ray, Is robed, yes, yes, yes, in bri-dal ar - ray.

Second.

Sun-beams glancing, brooklets danc-ing, Na-ture robed in bri - dal ar - ray, Is robed, yes, robed in bri - dal ar - ray.

304. Another interference with regular accent is sometimes caused by a *forzando* mark, thus (it may be called the accent of the forzando):

Allegretto.

Hap-py we, oh! hap · py we; Oh! hap-py, hap-py, hap-py we.

The forzando is *generally* used with accented beats.

305. Another setting aside of regular accent is sometimes caused by one of the rules of the slur or legato mark, which is, that when it connects two tones the first should be accented.

Moderato.

La, la, la, la, la, la, la, la.

Make the first of the two strong, the second light. But in all this irregular accentuation, the natural accent of the measure should be *felt* in the mind, as well as manifested by beats of the hand.

CHROMATIC TONES, MODULATIONS, AND MINOR KEYS.

The following lessons to be practiced after chromatic tones have been introduced. If the class have been accustomed to sing chromatic tones by imitation (See Normal Musical Hand-book, p. 98), these lessons will be easy to them. Name pitches before singing.

Something Passing Strange. (Round in three parts.)

do, re, mi, ri, mi, ri, mi, mi, fa, sol, fi, sol, fi, sol,
Here is something passing strange, That the key-tone does not change.

do, do, do, do, do, do, do, do, do, do, do, do.
D-sharp, F-sharp, full and free, Still in the key of C.

Pleasing Light and Shade. (Round in four parts.)

mi, ri, mi, re, do, sol, fi, sol, fa, mi,
Pleas-ing light and shade With these tones are made;

do, do, do, si, do, sol, sol, sol, do, sol, do.
They will bring no dis-cord here; You need not fear.

Three Things. (Round in four parts.)

do, re, ri, mi, fa, mi, mi, fa, fi, fi, sol, la, sol,
Three things are sought for, Pow'r, pleas-ure and wealth;

do, do, do, do, do, do, do, do, do, do.
One spoils our tem-per, And two spoil our health.

Glory Hallelujah. (Round in three parts.)

Chromatic tones.

sol, fi, sol, fi, sol, do, sol, fi, sol, fi, sol, mi, ri, mi, ri, mi, sol,
Glory hal-le-lu-jah, sing it o'er and o'er; Sing his love and mercy,

mi, ri, mi, ri, mi, do, do, do, mi, do, do, do.
sing it ev-er-more; Hum-bly wor-ship and a-dore.

Wintry Winds. (Round in three parts.)

Chromatic tones.

mi, fa, mi, fa, mi, re, do, sol, le, scl, le, sol, fa, mi,
Win-try winds are moan - ing, Win-try winds are moan - ing,

do, do, do, do, do, do, do, do, sol, sol, sol, sol, do, do.
But the sum-mer time is com-ing, Summer time is com-ing.

Comin' thro' the Rye.

Moderato.

do, di, re, ri, mi, fa, fi, sol, si, la, li, si, do,
1. If a bod - y meet a bod - y com - in' thro' the rye,
2. Ev-'ry las - sie has her lad - die, none they say have I;

do, si, se, la, le, sol, se, fa, mi, me, re, ra, do.
If a bod - y kiss a bod - y, need a bod - y cry?
Yet the lads all smile at me, when com - in' thro' the rye.

Universal Praise.

Although in the truest application of syllables, they should change where the key changes, still it is sometimes difficult to tell where the change of syllables should begin and end in a modulation, and often the modulation is very short. In these cases, it is common and allowable to treat the foreign tones as chromatic tones, and apply the syllables accordingly. Try both ways, as shown below.

Moderato.   Key of G.

mi, fa, mi, fa, mi, fa, mi,   la, la, sol, sol, sol, sol, sol, mi, fa,
                                   mi, mi, re, re, re, re, re.
1. Mu-sic, mu-sic ev-'ry-where,   In the earth and in the air, . .
2. In the brooklet's merry flow,   In the breez - es soft and low, . .

sol, la, sol, la, sol, la, sol, do, sol, do, do, si, re, fa, si, do,
                                               sol, sol, fi, la, do, fi, sol,
3. Mu-sic, mu-sic ev-'ry-where,   In the earth and in the air, . .

do, do, do, do, do, do, do,   fa, fa, sol, si, re, sol, do,
                                   do, do, re, fi, la, re, sol,

Key of C.   **Key of F.**   **Key of C.**

fa, fa, mi, mi, mi, fa, mi,   la, la, la, fa, fa, fa, mi.
                         si, la,

In the love-songs of the birds,   In the children's happy words.
In the earth and in the air,   Hear the mu-sic ev - 'rywhere.

sol, sol, sol, la, si, sol, sol, mi, do, mi, re, do, si, la, si, do.
                              do, do, la, fa,

Join we, then, our cho - rus raise,   With the u - ni - ver - sal praise.

sol, sol, do, do, do, sol, do,   fa, fa, sol, sol, sol, sol, do.
                         do,   la,

Never Mind.

ANON.

Where is F-sharp chromatic, and where diatonic, in this piece? Name pitches first.

Moderato.

1. What's the use   of al - ways fret - ting At   the tri - als we may find?
2. Trav - el   on - ward, work-ing, hop - ing; Cast no ling'ring glance behind
3. Fate may threaten, clouds may low - er, En - e-mies may be combined,

They are all   a - long our path-way, Trav - el on, and nev - er mind.
At   the tri - als once en - countered, Look a - head and never mind.
If   your trust in God   be stead - fast, He will help you, never mind.

The pitches of a Minor key are not all represented in the signature place. The pitch in every Minor key that is not in its relative Major key, is represented, when it is wanted, by means of an accidental.

306. Pitches of the key of A Minor in scale form.

Absolute.	A,	B,	C,	D,	E,	F,	G♯,	A,	G♯,	F,	E,	D,	C,	B,	A.
Relative.	1,	2,	3,	4,	5,	6,	7,	8,	7,	6,	5,	4,	3,	2,	1.
Syllable.	La,	si,	do,	re,	mi,	fa,	si,	la,	si,	fa,	mi,	re,	do,	si,	la.

307. E Minor,—relative to G Major.

E,	F♯,	G,	A,	B,	C,	D♯,	E,	D♯,	C,	B,	A,	G,	F♯,	E.
1,	2,	3,	4,	5,	6,	7,	8,	7,	6,	5,	4,	3,	2,	1.
La,	si,	do,	re,	mi,	fa,	si,	la,	si,	fa,	mi,	re,	do,	si,	la.

Relative Major and Minor keys are said to have the same signature.

308. B Minor,—relative to D Major.

B,	C♯,	D,	E,	F♯,	G,	A♯,	B,	A♯,	G,	F♯,	E,	D,	C♯,	B.
1,	2,	3,	4,	5,	6,	7,	8,	7,	6,	5,	4,	3,	2,	1.
La,	si,	do,	re,	mi,	fa,	si,	la,	si,	fa,	mi,	re,	do,	si,	la.

309. F-sharp Minor,—relative to A Major.

F♯,	G♯,	A,	B,	C♯,	D,	E♯,	F♯,	E♯,	D,	C♯,	B,	A,	G♯,	F♯.
1,	2,	3,	4,	5,	6,	7,	8,	7,	6,	5,	4,	3,	2,	1.
La,	si,	do,	re,	mi,	fa,	si,	la,	si,	fa,	mi,	re,	do,	si,	la.

Accidentals may reveal the fact that the staff represents the minor key.

310. D Minor,—relative to F Major.

D,	E,	F,	G,	A,	B♭,	C♯,	D,	C♯,	B♭,	A,	G,	F,	E,	D.
1,	2,	3,	4,	5,	6,	7,	8,	7,	6,	5,	4,	3,	2,	1.
La,	si,	do,	re,	mi,	fa,	si,	la,	si,	fa,	mi,	re,	do,	si,	la.

311. G Minor,—relative to B-flat Major.

G,	A,	B♭,	C,	D,	E♭,	F♯,	G,	F♯,	E♭,	D,	C,	B♭,	A,	G.
1,	2,	3,	4,	5,	6,	7,	8,	7,	6,	5,	4,	3,	2,	1.
La,	si,	do,	re,	mi,	fa,	si,	la,	si,	fa,	mi,	re,	do,	si,	la.

The last pitch in the base of any piece is key-tone, according to the usual rules of composition.

312. C Minor,—relative to E-flat Major.

C, D, E♭, F, G, A♭, B, C, B, A♭, G, F, E♭, D, C,
1, 2, 3, 4, 5, 6, 7, 8, 7, 6, 5, 4, 3, 2, 1.
La, si, do, re, mi, fa, si, la, si, fa, mi, re, do, si, la.

313. F Minor,—relative to A-flat Major.

F, G, A♭, B♭, C, D♭, E, F, E, D♭, C, B♭, A♭, G, F.
1, 2, 3, 4, 5, 6, 7, 8, 7, 6, 5, 4, 3, 2, 1.
La, si, do, re, mi, si, la, si, fa, mi, re, do, si, la.

314. Give relative names to the pitches of all these lessons before singing them. (The names of numbers are here relative names.)

la, si, do, re, mi, fa, mi, la, la, si, la, do, si, la,
Oft our words must plaintive be, Then we need the mi - nor key;

do, do, si, la, si, la, mi, mi, fa, mi, re, do, si, la.
Oft - en, too, in grief or pain, Will be heard this same sad strain.

315.

mi, la, si, la, si, do, si, la, si, la, si, do, re, mi,
1. When thou wert nigh the beam-ing sky Shone out in bright-er blue;
2. The brook-let's voice was sweet-er far, The song birds' trill more clear,

mi, fa, mi, re, re, mi, re, do, la, do, si, la, si, la.
When thou wert nigh the flow'rs of earth Took on a bright-er hue.
All na - ture wore a rich-er garb When thou, be-lov'd, wert near.

316.

mi, la, si, la, si, la, si, la, si, do, si, la, si, la,

1. The winds of au-tumn sad-ly sing The re-quiem of the flow'rs,
2. When all a-round seems dark and drear, Th'unbid-den tear may start;

mi, la, si, la, si, do, re, mi, fa, mi, re, do, si, la.

The bright hued birds have tak-en wing For soft-er skies than ours.
But wait and watch, the sky will clear If sum-mer's in the heart.

317.

la, si, la, mi, re, do, si, la, la, si, do, re, mi, fa,

Sad-ly the win-ter winds do blow, Cold is the earth 'neath the

mi, mi, la, si, la, si, la, mi, re, do, si, mi, la.

man-tle of snow, Si-lent the stream-let the ice be-low.

318.

la, do, si, la, si, la, si, mi, la, si, do, re, do, si, la,

1. O'er the hills the sun is set-ting, And an-oth-er day is gone;
2. Gone for aye, its race is o-ver, E-ven now the shades have come;

do, do, si, si, la, si, si, mi, la, si, do, si, la, si, la.

Slow-ly falls the gen-tle twi-light, Si-lent night is com-ing on.
But 'tis sweet to know at e-ven We are one day near-er home.

319.

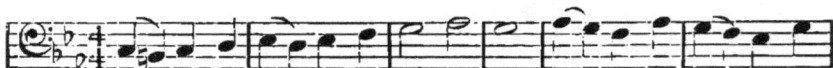

la, si, la, si, do, si, do, re, mi, fa, mi, fa, mi, re, fa, mi, re, do, mi,

Waves of the o-cean in sul-len roar, Moan for the friends that have

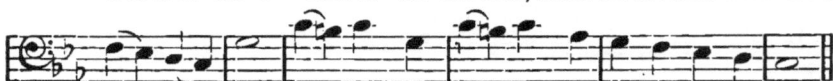

. re, do, si, la, mi, la, si, la, mi, la, si, la, fa, mi, re, do, si, la.

gone be-fore, Foam-ing and dash-ing up-on the rock-y shore.

GENERAL REVIEW.

What are the essential properties of every tone? What about a tone is called its length? What its pitch? What its power? What its quality? Give some illustration that will show what "quality of tone" means. What does the study of music really consist of? What are more concise terms than "the length of a tone, 'the pitch of a tone," etc.? Name the three departments in music. What things belong to Rhythmics? What to Melodics? What to Dynamics? When people speak of the rhythmic character of music, to what do they refer? When they speak of the melodic character of music, what is meant? What does "the dynamic character of music" refer to?

What are the pulsations called that the hand moves with in singing these lessons? Name the tone-length that goes here with each beat. What kind of note stands for the quarter length? What tone-length is as long as two beats? What is the name of the note that stands for the half-length? What are groups of beats called? What kind of measures consist of two beats? What represents measures to the eye? What kind of a bar closes a lesson? What motion of the hand goes with the first beat in double measure? What with the second? What are such motions of the hand called? In which department have we here been studying, Rhythmics, Melodics, or Dynamics?

To which department do tone-powers and tone-qualities belong, Rhythmics, Melodics, or Dynamics? What is the musical name for medium power? What is the abbreviation of mezzo? What is the name for a loud power? Abbreviation? For a soft power? Abbreviation? Very loud? Abbreviation? Very soft? Abbreviation? Is sadness in a tone a power or a quality? Is joyfulness a power or a quality? What are clear and somber? Which quality do gloomy words require? When no directions or marks on a piece show what powers and qualities are to be used, what indicates the proper ones to the singer?

What is the name of the low pitch that we have been singing to the syllable "do"? What is the name of the next pitch above C? Next above D? Next? Next? Next? Next? Next? What stands for the pitch C, treble staff? What kind of a note do we put on the line below if we wish that pitch sung one beat long? What kind of a note should we put on any line or space if we wanted its pitch sung two beats long? What is each line and space of the staff called? How many degrees has a staff of five lines? How many degrees has a staff of six lines? What figure stands for double measure? What is the note called that exactly coincides with each beat in a measure? What is beat-note in the foregoing lessons? What then constitutes their measure-sign? What does the measure-sign indicate or say? In what two departments are we singing when we use staffs and notes? Which is the Melodic character, the staff or the note? Which are Rhythmic characters, notes or staffs?

What are the names of letters as applied to tone-pitches, absolute or relative names? What are the names of numbers as used in music, absolute or relative names? What is the name of the character that makes the staff represent pitches in a new way? With the base clef which degree of the staff stands for C, or one? Is it the same "second space" that stood for A with the treble clef? Has the name of this space changed or is it its meaning or representation that has changed? With this clef upon the staff, which degree stands for D, or two? What pitch does this same "third line" stand for when the treble clef is upon the staff? What degree here stands for E, or three? For four? (Ask all the way up.) Under which head or in which department will you place the names of pitches and of the clefs— Rhythmics, Melodics, or Dynamics?

What are silences in music called? What is a rest as long as a quarter note called? What is a rest as long as a half note called? What are the characters or signs called that stand for these rests? In which department do rests belong?

When music makes its beats group themselves into threes, what kind of a measure is produced? Which is the accented beat of triple measure? Which are unaccented? Which of double measure? What is a length as long as three quarters called? What represents a dotted half to the eye? What figure stands for triple measure? What kind of note is beat-note in the lessons we have been singing? What is a moderate movement called? What is the name of the movement a little faster than moderato? What is the name of the silence that is as long as a dotted half note? What represents this silence to the eye? What is the measure-sign for the foregoing lessons?

What are four-beat measures called? What motions of the hand are used in beating time in this measure? Which are the accented beats? Which the unaccented beats? What new length have we used here? What new rest? On which side of a line is the whole rest placed? On which the half rest? What is the peculiarity of the whole rest? (It is used in any kind of measure as the measure rest.) What movement may be said to be the medium movement—neither fast nor slow? Name the faster movements in successive order, beginning with moderato. Name the slower movements in successive order beginning at the same place. (For pronunciation of movements, see page 4.) What figure stands for quadruple measure? What has been beat-note in the foregoing lessons? What, then, their measure-sign? In which department do movements belong, Rhythmics, Melodics, or Dynamics?

What are six-beat measures called? What motions of the hand are used for beating time in this measure? Which are the accented beats of this measure? What is the name of the length as long as six quarters? What is the name of the note that represents this length to the eye? What is the measure-sign for sextuple measure when the quarter is beat-note?

What is a key? What characteristics have the key-tones (one or eight) of a key? What are the characteristics of two of the family? Of three? Of five? Six? Seven? What syllable becomes associated with the repose of key-tone? What syllable with the more restless two? What with the peculiar character of three? What with the firm, restless four? What with the bold, restful five? What with the plaintive six? What with the bright, restless seven? Name the relative pitches of a key in regular order from key-tone to key-tone. Descending, from key-tone to key-tone. What is the name of the exercise or tune that is produced by singing these tones in the ascending or descending order? When key-tone is sung in connection with tones above it, is it one or eight? When sung in connection with tones below it which is it? To how many degrees is the treble staff enlarged in this chapter? How many the base staff? Name the degrees of each staff where the staff is largest. Place every name of tone or sign under its proper head (Rhythmics, Melodics, or Dynamics). What are the higher voices called? What are the lower voices called?

Name the absolute pitches that make the key of C. If F be dropped out from these tones, and F sharp substituted, what key will be the result? Name the pitches of the key of G. When the staff represents the key of C, what pitch does it represent that does not belong to the key of G? What can be done to the staff to stop it from representing F, and make it represent F sharp? What is the musical word for "sign of key"? What is the signature of the key of G?

What pitches constitute the key of D? Which of these pitches is not in the key of G? Which are not in the key of C? How is the staff made to stand for the pitches of the key of D? Can you tell when the staff is prepared for the key of C? Has it then a "sign of key"? When a line has a sharp upon it musicians say it is sharped, when it has a flat upon it they say it is flatted, when it has neither they say it is natural. What word would then best describe the condition of the signature place when the staff is prepared for the key of C? (The word "cancel" does not answer at all to describe this condition of the staff.)

Name the absolute pitches that make the key of A. What new pitch is here? How many degrees of the staff must be changed from "natural" in representing this key? How many must be left natural? Is it just as important that some should be "natural" as that others should be "sharped"? What is commonly said to be the signature of the key of A? What absolute pitch has the home or key-tone sound in this key? What relative name and character has this same A when used in the key of D? What is it in the key of G? What in the key of C?

What pitches constitute the key of E? How is the staff prepared to represent them? What is said to be the signature? What pitch in this key has the same character or mental effect that C has in the key of C? What in the key of E is like D in the key of C? What in E is like E in C? What in E is like F in C? What in E is like G in C? What in E is like A in C? What in E is like B in C?

What are the pitches of the key of F? What pitch has this key that the key of C has not? What degrees are natural and what flatted in preparing the staff for this key? What is the signature? What pitch in this family fills the office of home-tone or one? What pitch here plays the part of the restless two? What the plaintive three? (Question so of all. See page 26.)

What tones cluster around B-flat as key-tone? What degrees of the staff are natural and what flatted in representing this key? What pitch fills the office of domineering five in this key? Who is plaintive six? Who is restless seven? In what key is this restless A the plaintive six? In what key is it the bold five? In what key is it the reposeful key-tone? (Ask similar questions of other pitches of this key.)

What are the names of the tone-pitches that have E-flat for their home or key-tone? How is the staff arranged to represent this key? What is the character or mental effect of E-flat when heard in this key? What is the character of F when in this relationship? What G? What A-flat? What B-flat? What C? What D? Has D been restless seven in any previous key?

Name the pitches that cluster around A-flat as key-tone. What is a full description of the condition of the staff in the signature place, when it is prepared to represent the pitches of this key? Are the natural degrees as important as the flatted ones? What is the abbreviation, or common name, of signature? In how many of the nine keys that we have now sung in, is the pitch C used? In how many C sharp? In how many D? In how many D-flat? (Ask in this way of each absolute pitch.)

How many tone-pitches does it take to make an interval? When we hear C and D, do we hear a Step or a Major second? Which term describes the difference of pitch or distance between the two pitches? When we hear one and two of a key, do we hear a Major second or a Minor second?

NOTE TO TEACHER.—These questions have reference to Major keys.

When we hear two and three, do we hear a Major second or a Minor second? When we hear three and four, which? Four and five? Five and six? Six and

seven? Seven and eight? How far apart are one and two? Two and three?
Three and four? Four and five? Five and six? Six and seven? Seven and
eight? Which interval do E and F produce, a Major second or a Minor second?
How far apart are E and F? Which interval do E and F sharp produce? How
far apart are they? Which do A and B-flat produce? How far apart are they?
Which do A-flat and B-flat produce? How far apart are they? (Ask of other seconds, using absolute pitch-names.)

Which are called diatonic tones, the regular members of a key or strangers that
may be introduced temporarily into it? Which are chromatic tones? Name the
absolute pitches that are diatonic in the key of C. Name those that are diatonic
in the key of D. Name those of E. Of F. Of B-flat. Of A-flat. Name any
pitch that would be chromatic in the key of C. In the key of G. D. A. E. F.
B-flat. E-flat. A-flat. Take the absolute pitch C; is it diatonic or chromatic in
the key of C? Is it diatonic or chromatic in G? In D? In A? E? F? B-flat?
E-flat? A-flat? The pitch F-sharp; is diatonic or chromatic in C? G? (Go
through all the keys. Ask similar questions of other pitches.) How is the chromatic scale formed?

What is going to another key during a piece of music called? What then is a
phrase, or section, from another key so introduced, called? (The teacher will see
that a distinction is here made between "modulating" and "modulation.") Are
modulations represented in the signature place, or by accidentals? Do accidentals
then always help to represent chromatic tones, or in modulations do they represent diatonic tones of the key introduced? Are accidentals ever used "by acci-
dent"? Then, has the musical meaning of this word any of its common meaning
in it?

How many kinds of keys are there in music? Which are more cheerful, major
or minor keys? Which more plaintive or mournful? What pitch is omitted from
the key of C major in forming the key of A minor? What pitch is substituted?
Name the pitches of the key of A minor. What is said of the major and minor
keys that have the most tone-pitches in common? What is the relative minor of
the key of C major? What the relative major of A minor? What the relative
minor of G major? What pitch is omitted from G major in forming the key of
E minor? What is substituted? (Ask in this way of the other keys, and also for
the names of the pitches that compose each minor key.) Name each relative major
and minor key. What is said of each relative major and minor key in regard to
signature? Is the pitch that is peculiar of each minor key represented in the signature place, or by an accidental? Does the accidental in this case help to represent a chromatic or diatonic tone? (The regular members of minor keys are diatonic, the same as regular members of major keys are.) What interval do one and
two of any minor key make,—a major second or a minor second? Two and three?
Three and four? Four and five? Five and six? Six and seven? Seven and eight?
How-far apart are the tones of a minor second? Of a major second? Of an augmented second? ("Step-and-a-half" should here be regarded as *one* word, because
it measures one interval,—a *second*. We want *two* measuring intervals when we
measure a Minor *third*,—then we say "step" and "half-step;" *three* measuring intervals for a *fourth*, four for a *fifth*, etc.

When is a tone-length said to be syncopated? Does the accent of a syncopation
coincide with, or conflict with, the regular accent of measures? Under what other
circumstances is the regular accent of measures interfered with?

This be our Motto.

Arranged.

1. This be our mot-to wher-ev-er we may go, "Faithful, Firm and True."
2. Sing then to-geth-er, with voic-es glad and free, "Faithful, Firm and True."

Oh, may it ev-er a-bove our pathway glow,"Faithful, Firm and True."
And may the ech-o of ev-'ry bos-om be, "Faithful, Firm and True."

1st time. | 2d time.

{ Faith-ful in our friendships, Kind to all in need;
{ True in thought and ac-tion, True in word and [OMIT.] deed.
{ School-days now are pass-ing, Quickly pass-ing by;
{ Life is just be-fore us, Stern-er cares are [OMIT.] nigh.

CHORUS.

This be our mot-to wher-ev-er we may go, "Faithful, Firm and True." }
Oh, may it ev-er above our pathway glow,"Faithful, Firm and True." }

(93)

Resisting the Tempter.

B. R. H.

Moderato.

1st voice. Come, mer - ry lad, I am wait - ing for you; Come, take a
" Come, mer - ry lad, take a seat by my side; Po - ny is
" Come, mer - ry lad, take a walk, and we'll find Where swing the
" Walk - ing, and rid - ing, and row - ing, for you, Must they all

sail on the wa - ter so blue. 2d voice. Dear - ly I love on the
pranc-ing, I'll give you a ride. " Dear-ly I love a gay
. ma - ple blooms, red, in the wind. " Dear-ly I love where the
wait till the school hours are thro'? " Yes, and I'll go till the

riv - er to row, Blithe is the boat, but to school I must go.
gal - lop, you know; Po - ny trots well, but to school I must go.
spring-blossoms grow; Rambling is fine, but to school I must go.
last hour is done! Then, boys, hur-rah, for the play and the fun.

CHORUS.

Brave lit - tle he - ro, well done, well done for you! Thus will we

*(The chorus take up the words of the 2d voice
in every verse when they get here.)*

an - swer the wi - ly tempt-er, too. Dear - ly I love on the

riv - er to row; Blithe is the boat, but to school I must go.

Over the Snow.

R. S. TAYLOR.

1. O - ver an o - cean of beau - ti - ful snow,
2. Un - der a can - o - py gemmed with the light,
3. Min - gling our sing - ing with jin - gling of bells,

Mer - ri - ly O! mer - ri - ly O! Swift as a bird in its
Mer - ri - ly O! mer - ri - ly O! Speed we a - way on our
Mer - ri - ly O! mer - ri - ly O! O - ver the val - ley our

flight we go, Mer - ri - ly, mer - ri - ly O!
path - way bright, Mer - ri - ly, mer - ri - ly O!
mu - sic swells, Mer - ri - ly, mer - ri - ly O!

CHORUS.

Mer - ri - ly, mer - ri - ly O! Mer - ri - ly, mer - ri - ly O!

Swift-ly we go, Mer - ri - ly, mer - ri - ly O!

O-ver the snow . . . . .

Christmas Bells.

Arranged.

1. Oh, the bell-chimes sweetly pealing, Gently on the air they're stealing,
2. Hark! a simple lay they're chiming, Hear the wild confus-ion rhym-ing,
3. List again! those tongues are seeming With a thousand voic - es teem-ing,

Mer-ry, mer-ry Christmas bells, Mer-ry, mer-ry Christmas bells.
Mer-ry, mer-ry Christmas bells, Mer-ry, mer-ry Christmas bells.
Mer-ry, mer-ry Christmas bells, Mer-ry, mer-ry Christmas bells.

Joy and love they're now re-veal-ing, Puls-es throb in hope-ful feel-ing,
Now in scale me - lodious climbing, Then a low and silv'-ry tim-ing,
Tell - ing that a star is gleaming, Now from Judah's plain is beaming,

Mer-ry, mer-ry Christmas bells, Mer-ry, mer-ry Christmas bells.
Mer-ry, mer-ry Christmas bells, Mer-ry, mer-ry Christmas bells.
Mer-ry, mer-ry Christmas bells, Mer-ry, mer-ry Christmas bells.

Happy New Year.

Unison.

1. Hap-py new year! hap-py new year! hap-py new year! With the
2. Hap-py new year! hap-py new year! hap-py new year! Each a

sleigh bells chiming sweetly, As we're gliding on so fleet-ly; Oh! the
cheer-ful heart is bringing, And a voice to join the sing-ing; Oh! the

win-ter suits complete-ly for laugh and song, Hap-py new year! hap-py
hours are swiftly wing-ing in win-ter time, Hap-py new year! hap-py

new year! hap-py new year! Hear the bells jin-gle, jin-gle, jin-gle,

1st. **2d.**

jin-gle, jin-gle, jing! Hear the mer-ry, mer-ry bells, bells.

Canadian Boat Song.

T. Moore.

In rowing time.

1. Faint-ly as tolls the eve-ning chime, Our voic-es keep tune and our
2. Why should we yet our sail un-furl, There is not a breath the blue
3. U - ta - wa tide! this trembling moon Shall see us float o - ver thy

oars keep time,   Our voic-es keep tune and our oars   keep time.
wave to   curl;   There is not   a breath the blue wave   to   curl;
surg - es   soon;   Shall see us float o - ver thy surg - es   soon;

Soon as the woods on shore look dim, We'll sing at St. Ann's our parting hymn.
But when the wind blows off the shore, Oh, sweet-ly we'll rest our wear-y oar.
Saint of this green isle! hear our prayer, Grant us cool heavens and favoring air!

Row, brothers, row, the stream runs fast, The rap-ids are near and the
Blow, breezes, blow, etc.
Blow, breezes, blow, etc.

day - light's past, The rap-ids are near and the day - light's past.

D H. H.
Allegretto.

1. Now to the bo - som of the earth We give the seed which
2. How kind - ly moth - er earth re - ceives The treas - ure of the
3. Re - mem - ber, till - er, that the rain, The sun-shine, and the

heaven may bless With warm rains for its springing forth, Till it shall
farm - er's seed, And nurs - es it till ten - der leaves A-wake from
sum - mer dew Are His who makes the blooming plain Re-turn to

CHORUS.

grow to fruit - ful - ness.
pris - on - bond-age freed. A few short weeks will bring a - long The
glad'-den earth a - new.

rip - ened grain and har - vest song, The mer - ry, mer - ry,

mer - ry, mer - ry, mer - ry, mer - ry, mer -ry, mer -ry har - vest song.

Robin Red-Breast.

Arranged.

Not too fast.

1. "You're full of mis-chief, sir," I said To Rob-in Red-breast blithe and fat;
2. In songful speech he gai-ly said, His bos-om glow-ing like the morn,
3. 'Tis true, he toils a-mid the corn, And saves the crops from wasteful blight;
4. The Rob-in is my prince of pets, I wish him joy and length of days;

"You stole my cher-ries ripe and red, Now what have you to say to that?"
"I take my pay in cher-ries red For work-ing in your vines and corn."
He calls us up with songs at morn, And gives us hap-py songs at night.
He more than pays for all he gets, In hon-est toil and hymns of praise.

The Angel Patience.

✳

Andantino.

1. There walks a si-lent an-gel Thro' this our earth-ly home;
2. And in his eyes peace shin-eth, And gen-tle grace a-bides;
3. For ten-der-ly he leads thee Thro' all thy earth-ly way;

With com-forts for earth's sor-row, Our Lord hath bid him come.
He is the an-gel Pa-tience, Oh! fol-low where he guides.
And cheer-ful-ly he bids thee Hope for a bright-er day.

Words from Clark's "School Visitor." New arrangement of Words and Music.

1. Ah! now they fall in mil-lions, The rain drops all a-round;
2. A light and air - y treb - le They play up - on the stream,
3. Oh! 'tis a storm of mu - sic, And rob - ins don't in - trude,

They're dancing on the house tops, They're hiding in the ground;
And then the tune is qui - et, Like mu - sic in a dream;
If when the rain is wea - ry, They give an in - ter - lude.

They're fair - y like mu - si - cians, With an - y - thing for keys,
A - non the base is sounding, With - in the for - est caves,
It seems as if the warbling Of birds in all the bow'rs,

The roof, the doors, the windows, The fenc - es and the trees.
With al - to from the zeph-yrs, And ten - or from the waves.
Had gath-er'd in - to rain-drops, And come to us in show'rs.

Song of the Planets.

Note.—If this song is acted, let one stand in the centr for the Sun, and one or a group at proper distances for Mercury, Venus, Earth, Mars and th: :her planets, and as they sing, walk round the center one in a circle. The same words are sung each time, excepting the name of the planet, which is changed in order. Where the name is only one syllable add "now," as "Earth now moves," etc.

Moderato.

Oh, how stead-i - ly, true and or - der-ly, Mer-cu - ry moves round the

orb of day, Nev - er drear-i - ly, nev - er wea-ri - ly, Nev - er

tir - ed on his act - ive way; Al - ways cir - cle-ing round the
(her)

bril - liant Sun, Nev - er wea - ry as he jour-neys on. Oh, how
(she)

or-der-ly still they're cir-cle -ing, Clinging to their center, the orb of day.

GEO. F. ROOT.

Allegretto.

1. O'er prai-rie green and fair We're gal-lop-ing, gal-lop-ing on;
2. Thro' beds of love-ly flow'rs We're gal-lop-ing, gal-lop-ing on;

As free, as free as air, We're gal-lop-ing, gal-lop-ing on;
As rich as sum-mer bow'rs, We're gal-lop-ing, gal-lop-ing on;

Where'er we go no bounds a-rise, Ex-cept the blue and cloudless skies,
Tho' ev-'ry seed by na-ture's hand Was scatter'd o'er this good-ly land,

We're gallop-ing, gal-lop-ing on, We're gal-lop-ing, gal-lop-ing on, We're
We're gallop-ing, etc.

dim. **pp**

galloping, galloping, galloping, galloping, galloping, galloping on.

The Spring Time is Coming.

Allegro.

1. The spring time is com - ing, And we will be mer - ry, Tra,
2. Oh, spring time, sweet spring time, We joy - ful - ly greet thee, Tra,

la, la, la, la, la! Good-bye to De - cem - ber And
la, la, la, la, la! Old win - ter would not be Per-

Tra, la,

cold Jan - u - a - ry, Tra, la, la, la, la, la! And
sua - ded to meet thee, Tra, la, la, la, la, la! And

Tra, la,

while we are sing - ing The song birds are call - ing, Tra,
now he has gone Let us sing and be mer - -y, Tra,

la, la, la, la, la! Oh, sweet on the ear is Their
la, la, la, la, la! Good-bye to De - cem - ber And

Tra, la,

mel - o - dy fall - ing, Tra, la, la, la, la, la.
cold Jan - u - a - ry, Tra, la, la, la, la, la.

Tra, la.

There's Music in the Air.

G. F. R.

Moderato.

1. There's mu - sic in the air When the in - fant morn is nigh,
2. There's mu - sic in the air When the noontide's sul - try beam
3. There's mu - sic in the air When the twilight's gen - tle sigh

And faint its blush is seen On the bright and laughing sky.
Re - flects a gold - en light On the dis - tant mountain stream.
Is lost on eve - ning's breast, As its pen - sive beau - ties die.

Chorus 2d time pp.

Many a harp's ex - tat - ic sound, With its thrill of joy pro - found,
When be - neath some grateful shade Sor - row's ach - ing head is laid,
Then, oh, then, the loved ones gone, Wake the pure ce - les - tial song,

While we list en - chant - ed there To the mu - sic in the air.
Sweet - ly to the spir - it there Comes the mu - sic in the air.
An - gel voi - ces greet us there In the mu - sic in the air.

Out West.

From "Forest Choir." H. L. FRISBIE.

Allegretto.

1. There's a coun-try fam'd in sto - ry, As you've of - tentimes been
2. Once a man in An-dros-cog-gin, Or in some out-land-ish
3. Then he cross'd the roll-ing prai-ries, Stretching on-ward like the
4. Climbing o'er the Rock-y mountains, On he kept his wea-ry

told; 'Tis a land of might-y riv-ers, Run-ning
place, With a view to find this coun-try, To the
sea; "I am bound to find this coun-try, If there's
way, Till the broad Pa-ci-fic's wa-ters Right be-

o - ver sands of gold: The a - bode of peace and
west-ward set his face. He was wea-ry at Chi-
such a one," said he: So he swam the Mis-sis-
fore his vis-ion lay: Here he sat him down and

plen - ty, And with qui - et - ness 'tis blest! But this
ca - go, So he sat him down to rest; But 'twas
sip - pi, Then up - on Mis-sou-ri's breast, He ex-
pon-der'd, But for him there was no rest; "'Tis an

coun-try that's so fa-mous Is a-way off in the west.
on-ly there the cen-ter, Not the fa-bled gold-en west.
plor'd the wilds of Kan-sas For this coun-try in the west.
is-land, sure-ly," said he, This fair coun-try in the west.

CHORUS.

'Tis a-way off in the west, 'Tis a-way off in the west;

in the west, in the west;

Oh! I fear we ne'er shall find it, 'Tis so far off in the west.

5 So a vessel quick he builded,
  And the shore he left behind,
Sailing on with eager longings,
  Still this happy isle to find:
After many days, one morning
  He beheld the wish'd-for land;
Steering 'mid the shoals and breakers,
  Quickly reach'd the golden strand.

CHORUS.

6 From his gallant bark he landed,
  Wading thro' the curling foam,
With his eyes wide ope with wonder,
  For he found himself at home:
Then he learn'd that one forever
  Might go on and never rest;
Still they would not find this country,
  For 'tis always further west.

CHORUS.

It will be an excellent plan sometimes to have this sung as a song and chorus,—the song by a boy or girl, who can give the story distinctly and with proper expression.

National Song.

Arranged.

Maestoso.

1. Come and join us with hearts and with voices, On this day when a na-
2. Tell the world how the right was de-fend-ed, How the strug-gle for free-
3. May thy fu-ture, Co-lum-bia, be glorious, O-ver wrong and oppres-

tion re-joic-es; Tell a-gain in the song and the sto-ry,
dom was end-ed, How the tu-mult of war and com-mo-tion
sion vic-to-rious; May the star of thine em-pire as-cend-ing,

With the bu-gle, the trum-pet, the drum, Of the fame, the re-nown,
Found an ech-o far o-ver the sea, How the lands and the isles
Guide the wand'rer to free-dom and rest; May its light, ev-er pure,

and the glo-ry Of the land that we claim as our own.
of the o-cean Sent their sons to the home of the free.
nev-er end-ing, By the whole world be hon-ored and blest.

ELIZA COOK. *(May be sung as a Duet.)* † † †

1. Tell me not of sparkling gems, Set in roy-al di-a-dems;
2. Bring the tu-lip and the rose, While their brilliant beau-ty glows;
3. Ar-dent in its ear-liest tie, Faith-ful in its la-test sigh

You may boast your diamonds rare, Ru-bies bright, and gems so fair;
Let the storm-cloud fling a shade, Rose and tu-lip both will fade;
Love and Friendship, god-like pair, Find their throne of glo-ry there;

But there's a peer-less gem on earth, Of rich-er ray and pur-er worth;
But there's a flow'r that still is found When mist and darkness close a-round,
All proudly scorning bribe and threat, Naught can break there the seal once set;

'Tis price-less, but 'tis worn by few—It is, it is the heart that's true.
'Tis changeless, fadeless in its hue—It is, it is the heart that's true.
For all the e-vil gold can do, Can nev-er warp the heart that's true.

Shut the Door!

G. F. R.

Allegretto.

1. Shut the door!   Shut the door!   For the
2. Shut the door!   Shut the door!   But be

Shut the door   Shut the door!

wint'ry winds are blowing, and the frosty air is cold; Shut the door!
sure you shut not out the poor and wea-ry on his way; Shut the door!

Shut the door!

Shut the door!   How they make the windows rattle with their
Shut the door!   Give him shelter from the tem-pest, and a

Shut the door!

thousand voic-es bold. Roar, old Storm-King, out in the weath-er,
welcome here to stay. Roar, old Storm-King, out in the weath-er,

We are safe - ly sheltered, and your blast we do not fear, Howl around the door and the window, We will shut them closely, and you can not en-ter here.

Influence.

Moderato.

1. What if the lit-tle rain should say, "So small a drop as
2. What if a shin-ing beam of noon, Should in its foun-tain
3. Doth not each rain-drop help to form The cool, re-fresh-ing

I Can ne'er re-fresh those thirst-y fields, I'll tar-ry in the
stay, Be-cause its fee-ble light a-lone Can not cre-ate a
shower, And ev-'ry ray of light to warm And beau-ti-fy the

sky, I'll tar-ry in the sky, I'll tar-ry in the sky?
day? Can not cre-ate a day? Can not cre-ate a day?
flower? And beau-ti-fy the flower? And beauti-fy the flower?

NOTE.—Those singing the Echo should be in another room, and so shut up that when singing *forte* their voices will sound like an echo. The proper effect of the echo can be produced only in this way. If sung *pianissimo* in the same room the effect will not be the same.

First Division.   G. F. R.

Allegretto.   Cres.

1. Have you ev - er heard the ech oes That sleep in yon-der hill, Em-

Dim.   *2d Division.*

bow - ered in the greenwood So sha - dy and so still? Oh,

Cres.

yes, we've heard the ech - oes That sleep in yon - der hill, Em-

Dim.   *1st Division.*

bow - ered in the greenwood So sha - dy and so still. Will they

2d Division.

an-swer to our call, To our tones re - turn - ing sing? They will

ff All.   Echo.   pp

an-swer to our call, And sweet-est mu - sic bring. Ech - o, ech - o, ech - o, ech - o, An-swer us a - gain, An-swer us a - gain.

Full Chorus.
Maestoso.

Wake the ech - oes far and wide, From for-est, hill, and mountain side.

Let their soft-ened numbers flow Thro' the woods and vale be - low;

Wake the ech-oes, wake the ech-oes, Wake the ech-oes, wake the ech-oes,

Hear their soft-ened numbers flow Thro' the woods and vale be - low,

vale be - low; Thro' the woods and vale be - low, vale be - low.

The Letters at School.

ST. NICHOLAS.

Recitando.

1. One day the let-ters went to school, And tried to learn each oth-er;
2. B, C, D, E and J, K, L Soon jostled well their bet-ters;
3. Now, thro' it all, the Con-so-nants Were rud-est and un-couth-est,
4. But spiteful P said "Pooh for U!" (Which made her feel quite bitter,)
5. And smiling E, the rea-dy sprite, Said, "Yes, and count me double."

They got so mixed 'twas really hard To pick out one from t'other.
Q, R, S, T— I grieve to say— Were ver-y naughty let-ters.
While all the pret-ty Vow-el girls Were certain-ly the smoothest.
And, call-ing O, L, E to help, He real-ly trie' to hit her.
This done, sweet *peace* shone o'er the scene, And gone was all the troub-le!

A went in first, and Z went last; The rest all were between them—
Of course, ere long, they came to words—What else could be ex-pect-ed?
And simple U kept far from Q, With face demure and mor-al,
Cried A, "Now E and C come here! If both will aid a min-ute,
Meanwhile, when U and P made up, The Cons'nants looked about them,

K, L and M, and N, O, P— I wish you could have seen them.
Till E made D, J, C, and T De-cid-ed-ly de-ject-ed.
"Because," she said, "we are, we two, So apt to start a quar-rel!"
Good P will join in mak-ing peace, Or else the mischief's in it."
And kissed the Vowels, for you see, They couldn't do without them.

There is Beauty Every-where.

1. There is beau - ty in the skies at evening, There is beau - ty in the noon - day bright, There is beau - ty in the ra - diant morning, There is beau - ty in the si - lent night.

2. There is beau - ty in the roll - ing riv - er, There is beau - ty in the spark-ling rill, There is beau - ty in the lof - ty mountain, There is beau - ty in the ver-dant hill.

3. There is beau - ty in the joy - ous spring time, There is beau - ty when the bright leaves fall, There is beau - ty in the storms of win - ter, There is sum-mer beau - ty more than all.

Beau - ty, beau - ty ev-'ry-where, Beau - ty, beau - ty ev-'ry-where.

The Voice of the Grass.

Notice that this is sextuple, and not compound double, measure.   G. F. R.

Andantino.

1. Here I come, creeping ev-'ry-where, Creeping ev-'ry-where,
2. Here I come, creeping ev-'ry-where, Creeping ev-'ry-where,
3. Here I come, creeping ev-'ry-where, Creeping ev-'ry-where,

By ev-'ry dust-y road-side, Up-on the sun-ny hill-side,
You can not see me com-ing, Nor hear my low, sweet humming,
Where new made graves are closing, Above the dead re-pos-ing,

Close by the nois-y brook, In ev-'ry sha-dy nook;
Far in the star-ry night, Nor in the morn-ing light;
There in the spring I come, To deck each si-lent home;

Lo! I come, creeping ev-'ry-where, Creeping ev-'ry-where.
Still I come, creeping ev-'ry-where, Creeping ev-'ry-where.
Si-lent-ly creeping ev-'ry-where, Creeping ev-'ry-where.

Geo. F. Root.

Moderato.

1. Fair as the morn-ing, bright as the day, Vis - ion of beau -ty,
2. An - gel of slum-ber, bright as the day, Vis - ion of beau -ty,

fade not a - way; O - ver the mount-ain, o - ver the sea,
tar - ry for aye; Chase from the spir - it shad - ows of care,

CHORUS.

Come in my dreams to me. Far and wide the ech -oes roll a - long,
Leave but thy presence there.

While the day world sings its bus - y song; But what are

all its la - bors to me, Un - der the Dream-land tree?

Beautiful Dew-Drops.

Andantino.

1. Beau - ti - ful dew - drops, jew - els of light, Dropp'd from the crown of the god-dess of night, Flashing in chains of her mys-tic - al links, Blaz-ing in founts where the fire - fly drinks; Beau-ti - ful dew-drops, diamonds so rare, Spangle the locks of her dusk-y-brown hair.

2. Beau - ti - ful dew - drops, flash-ing at morn, Bright - er than gems in earth's di - a-dems worn, Rud-dy their light on the lil - y's cheek glows, Pearl-y they gleam from the heart of a rose; Beau-ti - ful dew-drops, gems from the sky, Tears on the lash of the flower's bright eye.

3. Beau - ti - ful dew - drops, fair - est of pearls, Bless - ing each bud where the drooping vine curls, Richer and pur - er your worth seems to me— Rich-er by far than the pearls of the sea; Beau-ti - ful dew-drops, shimmering bright, Sweet as the stars in their heaven - ly light.

Sing without instrument when the piece is learned.

Andantino.

†††

1. Leaf by leaf the ros - es fall, Drop by drop the springs run dry;
2. So in hours of deepest gloom, When the springs of glad-ness fail,
3. Some sweet hope to gladness wed, That will spring a - fresh and new,

One by one, be - yond re - call, Sum-mer's beau - ties fade and die;
And the ros - es in their bloom Droop like maid-ens wan and pale,
When grief's win-ter shall have fled, Giv - ing place to sun and dew;

But the ros - es bloom a - gain, And the springs will gush a - new,
We shall find some hope that lies Like a si - lent germ a - part,
Some sweet hope that breathes of Spring Thro' the wea - ry, wea - ry time,

In the pleas - ant A - pril rain, And the Sum-mer's sun and dew.
Hid - den far from care - less eyes, In the gar - den of the heart.
Bud-ding for its blos - som - ing In the spir - it's si - lent clime.

From " Palace of Song," by per.

The South Wind sings of hap - py springs, And bright-hued

sum - mers on their joy - ous way; The South Wind

tells of blos - som bells, And all the mer - ry, mer - ry meads of

May; The West Wind breathes of sun - set heaths, And crown - ed

glo - ries of the wood-land old; The West Wind flies from Au-tumn

skies, And sun-clouds o - ver-laid with shin - ing gold. The East Wind shrills o'er des - ert hills, The East Wind moans o'er sea-blanched

bones; The North Wind sweeps from crys - tal deeps, The North Wind

blows o'er drift - ed snows, o'er drift - ed snows, O'er drift - ed

snows; But oh! The South Wind sings of happy springs, And bright-hued

sum-mers on their joy - ous way; The West Wind breathes of sun - set

heaths, And sun - clouds o - ver - laid with shin - ing gold.

Tick, Tock, Hear the Clock!

Observe that 3d part here is written on the Treble Staff. Make the notes before the rests short.

1. In the morning, bright and rud-dy,
2. But of all its tin - y voic- es,
3. Always prompt and al-ways read - y,

Tick, tock, hear the clock! Tick, tock, tick, tock,

Call - ing us to cheer-ful stud - y, In the even - ing—
No one more the heart re - joic - es, Than this bright and
Al - ways bus - y, al - ways stead - y, May we learn to

tick, tock, tick, tock, tick, tock, .

school hours flown--Softly say-ing, "Now go home." In the evening—
wel-come lay, "Tick, tock, tick, go out and play." Than this blithe and
be as true As the clock, our work to do. May we learn to

tick, tock, tick, tock, tick, tock.

school hours flown—Soft - ly say - ing, "Now go home."
wel - come lay, "Tick, tock, tick, go out and play."
be as true As the clock, our work to do.

Allegretto.

1. Beau-ti-ful day! Farmers a-way! Gather the ripened grain, yes!
2. Beau-ti-ful day! Farmers a-way! For 'tis our happiest time, yes!

Work with a will! Out on the hill! Or on the wav-ing plain.
Rich is the field! Gold-en the yield! Joyful the rhythmic rhyme.

CHORUS.

Click, click, click, click, click, click, Bring out the reap - er, quick!

Clack, clack, clack, clack, clack, clack, Out on the yel - low track!

Beau-ti-ful day! Farmers a-way! Gath-er the gold - en grain.

Summer's Coming.

CLIO STANLEY.

1. Hark! hark! the meadow lark, In the dew-y fields upspring-ing! In her train the
2. Hush! hush! the merry thrush, Flying o-ver field and for-est, Sings and sings, the
3. Wake! wake! the house forsake, Hear the buds and blossoms calling, Lilies op'n-ing

sil-ver rain, Whispers to the bud and grain, Hark! the summer's com-ing!
whole day long, Round-e-lays of mer-ry song! Hark! the summer's com-ing!
white and fair, Ros-es burst-ing ev-'ry-where, Yes! the summer's com-ing!

The Jovial Farmer Boy.

Allegretto.

Arr. from "Trumpet of Reform."

1. A jo-vial far-mer boy I'll be, As free as birds that sing,
2. No place for me— the crowd-ed town, With pavements hard and dry,
3. The squirrel leap-ing from the limb, Up-on the tree-top high,

And car-ol forth my songs of glee A-mong the flow'rs of spring.
With lengthened streets of dust-y brown, And gloomy hous-es high.
The lark that soars with ma-tin hymn, Is not more gay than I.

I'll plow, and sow, and drive my team, Be - fore the ris - ing sun,
Where ev'ry boy must bound his ball Up - on a neigh-bor's ground,
I'll go and come a farm - er boy, From cit - y trammel's free,

I'll swim and sail in silv - 'ry stream, When all my work is done.
And ev - 'ry shout and ev - 'ry call Dis-turbs the folks a - round.
I'll live the life that I en - joy, A farm - er boy I'll be.

Interlude, to be whistled.

Accompaniment.

Repeat pp after last verse.

126

Far Up in the Blue.

Mrs. NELLY EATON.
Allegretto.

1. Now flit the birds from field and wood, While autumn winds blow high;
2. They come with ear - ly buds and blooms, With painted leaves they hie
3. So youth-ful hopes, if led a - right, When cares of life draw nigh,

To seek a - gain a sun-nier land, Far up in the blue they fly.
A - way from changing sum-mer haunts, Far up in the blue they fly.
Are like the birds when win - ter comes, Far up in the blue they fly.

REFRAIN.

Far up in the blue, Far up in the blue, Far up in the blue they fly.

A Little Boy's Speech.

In reciting style.

1. I've staid here watching all the folks, And heard the big boys crack their jokes,
   I've seen you laugh, and heard you cheer, I did not want to in - ter - fere;
2. I hope you've had a jol - ly time, It takes ten cents to make a dime;
   Birds in their lit - tle nests a - gree, And su-gar can-dy does with me;
3. I hope you like all you have heard; I did not hark to ev - 'ry word,
   For I was thinking all the time, How I should say my lit - tle rhyme;

But I did wish they would get through, And let me do my talk-ing, too.
Grandmother says it makes me sick, But I get bet-ter ver-y quick.
I've done it now, and feel all right; I hope you do so, too. Good night!

Angels Whisper.

Do not say "gentul." Keep the point of the tongue against the roof of the mouth, just back of the front teeth, while singing the last syllable of "gentle."

G. F. R.

1. An-gels whis-per low and sweet, "Oh, be gen-tle, oh, be true;"
2. To the sad and err-ing one, "Oh, be gen-tle, oh, be true;"
3. List the whisper, low and sweet, "Oh, be gen-tle, oh, be true;"

May we hear the words they speak, Hear and heed them, too.
Ev-'ry deed of kind-ness done, Joy will bring to you.
Let it guide the wea-ry feet, All the jour-ney through.

REFRAIN.

Be gen-tle, be gen-tle, be gen-tle, kind and true,

Be true,

Be gen-tle, be gen-tle, Be gen-tle, kind and true.

Swissland, Swissland.

Moderato.

1. Swiss - land! Swiss - land! Home of
2. Swiss - land! Swiss - land! Thy dear

La, la, la, la, la, la, la, la, la, la, la, la, la, la, la, la, la, la, la, la,

beau - ty, Shall we nev - er see thee more?
mem - 'ry, Nev - er in my breast shall wane;

La, la, la, la, la, la, la, la, la, la, la, la, la, la, la, la, la, la, la, la,

Seas are roll - ing wide be - tween us,
Ere I die, whate'er be - tide me,

la, la, la, la, la, la, la, la, la, la, la, la, la, la, la, la,

We are on a for - eign shore.
To thee I'll re-turn a - gain.

la, la, la, la, la, la, la, la, la, la, la, la, la, la, la, la.

REFRAIN.

Swiss - land, Swiss - land, Home of beau - ty,

Switzerland, dear Switzer-land, Thou far off home, so beau-ti - ful, Oh,

Shall we nev - er see thee more?

shall we see thy loft - y peaks And verdant val-leys nev - er more?

My Mountain Home.

Giojoso.

1. Home, my own dear mountain home, Joy - ous - ly to thee I come.
2. 'Round my mountain home the breeze Wakes sweet music in the trees,
3. Once more in my mountain home, Ne'er from thee a - gain to roam,

Where each peak, with wintry snows, And each tree, where herds repose,
And the ech-oes' mel-low swell, Where be - lov - ed kindred dwell,
Where each scene so grand, so fair, On the earth and in the air,

REFRAIN.

home, . . . tell, etc.

Tell of thee, my mount - ain home. Tell of thee, tell of

home, . tell, etc.

thee, my mountain home. Tell of thee, tell of thee, my mountain home.

Short Speech Sufficeth.

Moderato.

1. Short speech suf - fic - eth Deep tho'ts to show, When you with
2. Save me from speech - es Long, dull and slow, Oh! how much
3. Time nev - er lin - gers, Moves nev-er slow, While he per-

yes, or no, yes, or no,

wisdom say yes, or no, yes, or no, yes, or no.
better plain yes, or no, yes, or no, yes, or no.
mits it say yes, or no, yes, or no, yes, or no.

Hear the First Clear Song.

Moderato.

1. Hear the first clear song of the mav - is in the morn! He is
2. How the work flies on thro' the mer - ry summer day, For the
3. Still the same blithe song when the twilight shadows fall, As it

pip - ing to the boys while they're working in the corn; How the
will-ing hands are strong, and the happy hearts are gay; And the
mingles with the sound of the farm-er's welcome call; Then the

wood - lands ring thro' their arch - es all a - round, As they
time goes fast in the field so wide and free, As they
ech - oes wake in the wood-land once a - gain, As they

whistle back the joyful sound, As they whistle back the joyful sound.
whistle back the mel-o - dy, As they whistle back the melo - dy.
whistle back the glad refrain, As they whistle back the glad refrain.

Interlude, to be played on instruments or whistled.

After last verse repeat pp.

The River's Laughing Song.

G. F. R.

G. F. Root.

Allegretto. Clear tone.

1. From my win - dow you may see How the riv - er winds a - long,
2. Thro' the mead - ow, by the mill, Rip-pling onward mer-ri- - ly,
3. Floods of sun - ny gold - en light, 'Mid the laughing wavelets play,

With its love - ly sun - lit wave, And its ev - er laughing song.
Swelled by many a tin - y rill, Flows the riv - er to the sea.
And a mil - lion rain-bows bright Glit - ter in its dia-mond spray.

CHORUS.

You may see it glanc-ing, dancing, Now re - ced-ing, now ad - vanc-ing,

You may hear it ring-ing, sing-ing, As it murmurs on its way;

You may see its crys - tal flash - ing, Where the peb-bles keep it dash-ing, To the mu - sic of its plash-ing all the day.

Sparkling Water.

Moderato.

1. Come, let us sing of fount and spring, Of brooklet, stream, and riv - er,
2. Down fall the show'rs to feed the flow'rs, And in the sum - mer, nightly,
3. Each lit - tle bird whose song is heard Thro' grove and meadow ringing,

And tune our praise to him always, The good and gracious Giv - er.
The blos - soms sip with ros - y lips The dew-drops gleaming brightly.
At stream-let's brink will blithely drink, To tune its voice for sing-ing.

CHORUS.

No drink can e'er with this com - pare, For ev - ery son and daugh - ter,

The sweet-est draught that can be quaffed Is wa - ter, sparkling wa-ter.

The Old-Fashioned Watchman. G. F. ROOT.

Let the watchman's voice recede each time—the last cry of each hour being far in the distance.

Moderato.

1. Hear the voice of the watchman pro-claim-ing the hour,
2. Hear the voice of the watchman pro-claim-ing the hour,
3. Hear the voice of the watchman pro-claim-ing the hour,
4. Hear the voice of the watchman pro-claim-ing the hour,

Twelve o'-
One o'-
Two o'-
Three o'-

Hark! hark! Still-er now is the noise and the
Hark! hark! 'Tis a time when the gay and the
Hark! hark! How the mo-ments glide on in their
Hark! hark! See the beams of the morning now

clock! twelve o'clock!
clock! one o'clock!
clock! two o'clock
clock! three o'clock!

tu - mult of day, While the voice of the watchman is
glad ones may sleep, But the wea - ry must watch, and the
cir - cles a - way, Soon the night will be lost in the
faint - ly a - rise, How they gild with their beau - ty the

Dim.

far - ther a - way. Hear! . . . .
wretched must weep. Hear! . . . .
splendor of day. Hear! . . . .
blue e - ther skies. Hear! . . . .

p   pp   Dim.

Twelve o'-clock! twelve o'-clock! twelve o'-clock!
One o'-clock! one o'-clock! one o'-clock!
Two o'-clock! two o'-clock! two o'-clock!
Three o'-clock! three o'-clock! three o'-clock!

Ten Little Fairies. (A Song for Little Girls.) 135

M. B. C. SLADE.

(At the closing couplet let all the little hands unclasp, and all the fingers twist about, raised high above the head.)

Allegretto.

1. Do you think there are no fair-ies? Do you think the Fair-y Queen
2. In sweet sum-mer, when the air is Full of fra-grance of the flow'rs
3. When the autumn days of glo-ry Ripen'd fruits in clus-ters fling.
4. That kind works of love and du-ty, In the home, and in the school
5. Soft-ly sound our tune-ful numbers, For they now are drawing near,

On mid-sum-mer night no where is In the moonlight to be seen?
Then our bus-y lit-tle fair-ies Seek the sha-dy dells and bow'rs,
Then the fair-ies of our sto-ry Grapes and apples to us bring;
Are the on-ly way of beau-ty, Is our fair-ies' gold-en rule;
Wak-ing up from qui-et slumbers, Soon our fair-ies shall ap-pear;

Hear the sto-ry we are tell-ing, Ten with us are al-ways dwell-ing,
And they bring us pret-ty po-sies, Lil-ies, vio-o-lets and ro-ses;
And when soft white snow is fall-ing, At the mer-ry chil-dren's call-ing,
In what-ev-er work their share is, More and more we hope their care is
Now each queen will forward bring her's, Not one sin-gle fair-y lin-gers!

Ere our song has ceas'd its swell-ing You shall see them, by and by.
Ere our fair-y sto-ry clos-es You shall see them, by and by.
They will join the gay snow-ball-ing, You shall see them, by and by.
To be faith-ful lit-tle fair-ies, You shall see them, by and by.
They are—just our ten white fin-gers, Don't you see them dancing by?

Beauty Lingers Every-where.

Moderato.

1. Beau - ty lin - gers ev - ery-where a - round us, In the mys - tic
2. Beau - ty is but our Cre - a - tor's pres-ence, Shin - ing dim - ly

shade, and mead-ow fair; Beau-ty's charm to ev - ery scene hath bound us,
thro' the earth - ly thing; He of beau - ty is the soul and es - sence,

In the teem - ing earth or am - bient air. Beau - ty,
Then to him our joy - ful prais-es sing.

Beau - ty,

beau - ty, Beau - ty lin - gers ev - ery - where. . . .

beau - ty ev - ery-where.

Beau-ty, beau-ty, Beau-ty lin-gers ev - ery - where.

Beau-ty, beau-ty,

Whistle and Hoe.

Allegretto.

1. There's a boy just o - ver the gar - den fence, Who is whistling a-
2. Not a word be - moaning his task I hear; He has scarcely the
3. But then while you whis-tle be sure to hoe, For if i - dle the

long thro' the live - long day; And his work is not just a
time for a growl, I know; For his whis - tle mer - ry sounds
bri - ars will thrive and spread; And the whis - tle on - ly through-

mere pre-tense, For you see all the weeds he has cut a - way.
out so clear, He must find it some pleasure in ev - ery row.
out the row, May do well for the weeds, but is bad for the bread.

REFRAIN.   Repeat pp

Whistle and hoe, whistle and hoe, Shorten the row by the songs you know.

(To be whistled.)

Join 2d and 3d verses closely to this interlude.

Oh, Glorious Land.

From "School of Singing," by per.

Maestoso.

1. Oh, glo-rious land, with love o-verflow-ing, Joy-ful we
2. Fore-most of all in pro-gress thy sta-tion, Home of th' op-

sing thy fame so brightly glow-ing; Wher-e'er on high thy
pressed from each down-trodden na-tion, On scroll of fame thy

col-ors are fly-ing, There are thy chil-dren safe, on thee re-
sons' names shall clus-ter, And e'er thy his-t'ry shine with brightest

ly-ing. Are oth-er lands fair - er than thou art?
lus-ter. When from a-far home-ward we re-turn,

lands more fair than thou art?
a-far we home-ward turn.

Still thou art home, and there dwells the heart. Then, oh, glo-rious
How thrills the heart, how our love doth burn. Then, etc.

land, with love o - ver-flow - ing, Joy - ful we sing thy

fame so brightly glow - ing, Thy fame so brightly glow - ing,

glo - rious land, Thy fame so brightly glow - ing, glo - rious land.

Oh, Broad Land, Oh, Fair Land.

Maestoso. Dim.

1. Oh, broad land, oh, fair land, Oh, land that gave us birth,
2. We hon - or and praise thee, Oh, realm en-rich'd by heav'n,
3. For free-dom, for knowl-edge, A - like to great and small,
4. Oh, broad land, oh, fair land, Oh, land that gave us birth,

Oh, near land, oh, dear land, Our home of all on earth.
We love thee, we bless thee, For price-less bless - ings giv'n.
For care and pro - tec - tion, And e - qual rights to all.
Oh, near land, oh, dear land, Our home of all on earth.

The Three Bumble Bees.

All should practice singing from the Base clef. If convenient, let boys sing this base. Without instrument, after the piece is learned.

Arranged.

Allegretto.

1. There were three buzz - ing bum - ble bees, three buzz-ing bum - ble bees;
2. There were three buzz - ing bum - ble bees, three buzz-ing bum - ble bees;

Try and have the three parts sung.

They swept the gar - den all the day, With their zoom, zoom, zoom, zoom,
They swept the gar - den all the day, With their zoom, etc.

zoom, zoom, zoom, zoom, zoom, zoom, zoom, zoom, zoom, zoom, zoom, zoom,

1. And ev - 'ry flow'r they set - tled in, Just
2. They sang and buzzed till night came on, And

zoom, zoom, zoom, zoom, zoom, zoom, zoom, zoom, zoom, zoom, zoom, zoom,

shook its sides to hear the merry din, And all the leaves the
eve - ning breez - es quivered chill and lone, But to the last the

zoom, zoom, zoom, zoom, zoom, zoom, zoom, zoom, zoom, zoom, zoom, And
But

gar - den round, Kept laughing at the dron-ing sound, **zoom,**
gar - den round, Kept laughing at the dron-ing sound,

all the leaves the gar - den round, Kept laugh-ing at the
all the leaves the gar - den round, Kept laugh-ing, etc.

zoom, zoom, zoom, zoom, zoom, zoom, zoom, zoom, zoom, zoom, zoom, zoom, zoom,

1st time.   2d time.

sound, Kept laugh-ing at the sound, zoom, zoom, zoom. sound.

zoom, Kept laugh - ing at the sound.   And
They

The Honey Seekers.

At the letter Z, let the lower Alto make a continuous sound, with the teeth together, as if commencing the word "Zeal." ✱

Allegretto.

1. The bees, the bees are all com - ing, O why, O why are they humming?
2. Oh, see them now in the gar - den, A-like all bearing a bur - den.
3. They fly, they fly to the mead - ow, In sun-light and in the shad - ow;

O - ver each flower Of the green bower, Honey they seek, Honey they seek.
Where in each flower Of the green bower Honey they seek, Honey they seek.
Still in each flower Of the green bower Honey they seek, Honey they seek.

Repeat, with very soft power.

See! See! See! See! Hon-ey they seek, Hon-ey they seek.

Z . . . . .

Time Flies.

The words must often indicate the power and quality to be used.

Moderato.

1. We are but minutes,—lit - tle things, But ev -'ry one is
2. We are but min-utes, use us well, For ev -'ry min-ute's

furnished with six - ty wings, With which we swiftly fly on our
use you must one day tell ; Who us- es well the min-utes, has

un - seen track, And not a min - ute ev - er comes back.
hours to use, Who los - es min - utes, years may lose.

The Road to Slumber-Land.

Accommodate the music of the first verse to second and third verses, according to indication.
Words from " The Nursery," by per.

GEO. F. ROOT.

P **Andantino.**

1. What is the road to Slum-ber-land, and when does the ba - by
2. Two lit - tle tir - ed satin - y feet from the shoe and the stocking
3. And close and closer the blue-veined lids are hid - ing the ba - by

go?   The road lies straight thro' mother's arms, when the sun is sinking
free.   Two little palms to - gether pressed at the pa-tient mother's
eyes—   As over the road to Slumber-land the dear little trav'ler

low;   He goes by the drows-y "land of nod"; to the
knee;   Some ba - by words that are drowsi-ly lisped in the
bies;   And this is the way, thro' moth-er's arms, the

mu - sic of "lul - la - by,"   When all wee lambs are
ten - der Shep-herd's ear,   And a kiss that only a
pre - cious dar - lings go   To the beautiful city of

safe in the fold, un - der the eve - ning sky.
moth-er can place on the brow of her ba - by dear.
Slum - ber-land, when the sun is sink - ing low.

The Star Spangled Banner.

NATIONAL SONG.

Maestoso.

1. Oh, say can you see by the dawn's ear - ly light,
2. On the shore dim - ly seen thro' the mists of the deep,
3. And where is that band who so vaunt - ing - ly swore
4. Oh! thus be it ev - er when free - men shall stand

What so proud - ly we hailed at the twilight's last gleaming;
Where the foe's haughty host in dread si - lence re - pos - es,
That the hav - oc of war and the bat - tle's con - fu - sion,
Be - tween their lov'd home and the war's des - o - la - tion;

Whose broad stripes and bright stars thro' the per - il - ous fight,
What is that which the breeze o'er the tow - er - ing steep,
A home and a coun - try shall leave us no more?
Blest with vic - t'ry and peace, may the heav'n-rescued land

O'er the ram-parts we watch'd, were so gal-lant - ly streaming?
As it fit - ful - ly blows, half con-ceals, half dis - clos - es?
Their blood has washed out their foul footsteps' pol - lu - tion;
Praise the Power that has made and pre-served us a na - tion;

And the rock - et's red glare, the bombs bursting in air,
Now it catch-es the gleam of the morn-ing's first beam,
No ref - uge can save the hire - ling and slave,
Then con - quer we must, when our cause it is just,

Gave proof thro' the night that our flag was still there;
In full glo - ry re - flect - ed now shines in the stream;
From the ter - ror of flight or the gloom of the grave.
And this be our mot - to, "In God is our trust."

Oh, say, does the star spangled ban - ner yet wave,
'Tis the star spangled ban - ner, oh, long may it wave,
And the star spangled ban - ner in tri - umph shall wave,
And the star spangled ban - ner in tri - umph shall wave,

O'er the land of the free, and the home of the brave?
O'er the land of the free, and the home of the brave.
O'er the land of the free, and the home of the brave.
O'er the land of the free, and the home of the brave.

Who?

The duet may be sung by different single voices, or sections.
"GUERALL."
DUET.

1. Who paints the sun - set's blaz - ing light? Who draws the deep dark shades of night?
2. Who gives the fra - grant floweret birth, The sweet and ten - der things of earth?
3. Who makes the clinging, strengthless vine Round stronger, firm - er trunks en-twine?
4. Who makes the riv - er ebb and flow? Who sends the rain and drops the snow?

Who lifts the veil from morning's hour, And shows the earth a flow-'ring bower?
Who makes the oak from a - corn shoot, That fu - rious storms can ne'er up - root?
In spring-time who the leaves un - fold— Who scat - ters them in au - tumn cold?
Who gave the sun, and moon's soft light? Who sends the day, who sends the night?

CHORUS.

'Tis God in Na - ture's vast ex-tent! 'Tis Na - ture's God, Om-nip - o - tent!

Gathering Home.

By per. of Messrs. S. BRAINARD'S SONS.

Let all become familiar with singing from the base staff.
Andantino.
Cres.

1. The sun - set fades a - long the hills; Floods of gold - en light
2. The hunts-men ride a - long the hills In the gold - en light,
3. Oh, soon for us no more shall be Morn or eve - ning light,

Dim. *p* *Cres.*

Dy - ing in - to night; Soft twi - light now the val - ley fills;
While the com - ing night, From spir - it wings, the dew dis - tills;
Earth-ly noon or night; But death's un - fathom'd mys - te - ry,

Dim the shad-ows fall O - ver all;
Bid - ding qui - et fall O - ver all;
Set - tling like a pall O - ver all;

Hark! hark! the song the
Hark! hark! the huntsmen's
Then if the gold - en

o - ver all

reap - ers sing, As they gath-er home, Blithely gath - er home; Hark!
wind - ing horn, As they gath-er home, Blithely gath - er home; Their
harps we hear, As we gath-er home, Safe - ly gath - er home, We'll

how the vales and woodlands ring, As the ech-oes sweet loud - ly call.
tones on twi-light zeph-yrs borne, As the ech-oes sweet soft - ly call.
know our Father's throne is near, And for us the sweet heav'nly call.

REFRAIN.

Oh, hear the strain, Gath'ring home, gath'ring home.

Oh, hear the joy-ful strain, Gath'ring home, gath'ring home;

Oh, hear the strain Gath'ring home, gath'ring home.

Oh, hear the joy-ful strain, Gath'ring home, gath'ring home.

Better Late than Never.

Arranged.

m **Allegretto.**

1. This life's a race where some succeed, While oth-ers are be - gin - ning;
2. Oh, do not work for i - dle boast Of vic-t'ry o'er an - oth - er,
3. Choose well the path in which you run, Succeed by no - ble dar - ing;

'Tis luck at times, at oth-ers speed, That gives us ear - ly win - ning;
But while you strive your uttermost, Deal fair-ly with your broth - er;
Then when at last the crown is won, It will be worth the wear - ing;

cres. *f* dim.

But if you chance to fall be-hind, Ne'er slacken your en - deav - or;
Whate'er your station, do your best, And hold some purpose ev - er,
Then nev-er fret if left be-hind, Nor slacken your en - deav - or,

m *f*

But keep this wholesome truth in mind, "'Tis bet-ter late than nev - er."
And if you fail to beat the rest, "'Tis bet-ter late than nev - er."
But ev - er keep this truth in mind, "'Tis bet-ter late than nev - er."

All Aboard.

G. F. R.

DUET.

1. The skies are now bright, The wind is a-right,
2. A bird on the wing, The "Sea - Foam" will fling
3. Each sail is now taut, This breeze is as nought,

CHORUS.

DUET.

Up, up with the anchor, boys, do not de-lay; Oh, heave, there she
The white spray above us, o'er bowsprit and prow; We fly o'er the
On rig-ging so strong, and so fresh, and so new; The tide is at

CHORUS.

goes, The breeze, there she blows; The sails are all fill-ing, and
wave, Each breath we must save, Tho' swiftly the wa-ter comes
flood, Come, sea - ward we'll send. Hurrah for the "Sea-Foam," our

we are a-way, Yes, the sails are all fill-ing, and we are a-way.
o - ver the bow, Yes, tho' swift-ly the wa-ter comes o-ver the bow.
clip-per so true! Yes, hurrah for the "Sea-Foam," our clipper so true!

Yo ho! Yo ho! All fill-ing, all fill-ing, and we are a-way.
Yo ho! Yo ho! Tho' swiftly, tho' swiftly it comes o'er the bow.
Yo ho! Yo ho! Our clipper is gal-lant, is gal-lant and true.

Watchwords.

These solos may be sung by single voices.

G. F. Root.

1. *Hope* while there's a hand to work! *Dare* while there's a young heart brave;
2. *See* that there's a work for each! *Learn* that there is strength in God;
3. *Love* when there's a foe that wrongs; *Help* when there's a broth - er's need;

Toil while there's a task unwrought; *Trust* while there's a God to save. Yes,
Know that there's a crown re-served; *Wait*, tho' 'neath the cloud and rod. Yes,
Watch when there's a tempt-er near; *Pray*, both in thy word and deed. Yes,

Hope! dare! toil! trust! These are watchwords true and just, These are
See! learn! know! wait! These are watchwords true and great, These are
Love! help! watch! pray! Let us all these words o - bey, Let us

watch-words true and just, These are watch-words true and just.
watch-words true and great, These are watch-words true and great.
all these words o - bey, Let us all these words o - bey.

Con Spirito.

1. In the quar - ries do you toil—Make your mark; Do you
2. In the strife for learn-ing's prize—Make your mark; If in
3. Life is fleet - ing as a shade—Make your mark; Marks of

work up - on the soil? Make your mark! In what-ev - er path you
ear - nest to be wise—Make your mark; In your schoolday's precious
some kind *must* be made—Make your mark; Make it while the arm is

go, In what - ev - er place you stand—Moving swift or mov - ing slow—
hours, Or in af - ter search for fame, Keep in ac - tion all your pow'rs,
strong, In the gold - en hours of youth: Never, nev - er make it wrong;

With a firm and honest hand—Make your mark! Make your mark! Make your mark!
For a good and noble name; Make your mark! Make your mark! Make your mark!
Make it with the stamp of *truth*—Make your mark! Make your mark! Make your mark

The Corn Song.

JOHN G. WHITTIER.   Arranged.

Moderato.

1. Let oth - er lands ex - ult - ing, glean The ap - ple from the pine,
2. Thro' vales of grass and meads of flowers Our ploughs their furrows made,
3. All thro' the long, bright days of June, Its leaves grew green and fair,

The or - ange from its glos - sy green, The clus - ter from the vine;
While on the hill the sun and showers Of change-ful A - pril played;
And waved in hot mid-summer's noon Its soft and yel - low hair;

We bet - ter love the hard - y gift Our rug-ged vales be - stow,
We dropped the seed o'er hill and plain, Be-neath the sun of May,
And now, with Autumn's moonlit eves, Its har-vest time has come,

To cheer us when the storm shall drift Our har - vest fields with snow.
And frightened from our sprouting grain The rob - ber crows a - way.
We pluck a -way the frost - ed leaves, And bear the treas - ure home.

The gold-en corn, the gold - en corn, We sing the gold - en corn.
The gold-en corn, the gold - en corn, We sing the gold - en corn.
The gold-en corn, the gold - en corn, We sing the gold - en corn.

Tell the story distinctly. *The lengths of the notes may be changed a little, to accommodate the pronunciation of the words.* ✻

Recitando.

1. A fool-ish lit-tle maid-en bought a fool-ish lit-tle bonnet,
2. But tho' the lit-tle bon-net was scarce larg-er than a dime,
3. So this foolish lit-tle maid-en stood and wait-ed at the door;

With a rib-bon, and a feath-er, and a bit of lace up-on it;
Yet the get-ting of it set-tled prov'd to be a work of time;
And she shook her ruf-fles out be-hind, and smoothed them down be-fore;

And that all the oth-er maid-ens of the lit-tle town might know it,
So when it was fair-ly read-y, all the bells had stopp'd their ringing,
"Halle-lu-jah! Hal-le-lu-jah!" sang the choir a-bove her head,

7 She tho't she'd go to meet-ing, as the prop-er place to show it.
7 And when she came to meet-ing, sure e-nough the folks were singing.
"Hardly knew you! hardly knew you!" were the words she tho't they said.

4 This made the little maiden then so very, very cross,
That she gave her little mouth a twist, her little head a toss;
For she thought the very hymn they sang, was all about her bonnet,
With the ribbon, and the feather, and the bit of lace upon it.

5 And she would not wait to listen to the sermon or the prayer,
But pattered down the silent street and hurried up the stair,
Till she reached her little bureau, and in a bandbox on it,
Had hidden safe from critic's eye, her foolish little bonnet.

6 Which proves, my little maidens, that you each will surely find
In every Sabbath service but an echo of your mind;
And that the little head that's filled with silly little airs,
Will never get a blessing from the sermons or the prayers.

Over and Over Again.

F. W. Root.

1. O-ver and o-ver a-gain the brook thro' the mead-ow flows, And
2. O-ver and o-ver a-gain, no mat-ter which way I turn, I

o-ver, and over, and o-ver a-gain, The tire-less mill wheel goes;
always may find in the great book of life Some lesson I have to learn;

So the dews of morning must fall, And the sun, and the summer rain
I must take my turn at the mill, While it grinds out the golden grain,

Must do their part, and per-form it all O-ver and o-ver a-gain.
Must do my task with a right good will, O-ver and o-ver a-gain.

Must do their part, and perform it all O-ver and o-ver a-gain.
Must do my task with a right good will, O-ver and o-ver a-gain.

Home, Sweet Home.

Favorite Melody.

Andante.

1. 'Mid pleas-ures and pal - a - ces tho' we may roam, Be it
2. An ex - ile from home, splen-dor daz - zles in vain; Oh,

ev - er so hum - ble, there's no place like home. A charm from the
give me my low - ly thatch'd cottage a - gain, The birds sing-ing

skies seems to hal-low us there, Which, seek thro' the world, is ne'er
gai - ly, that come at my call; Give me these, with the peace of mind

met with else - where. Home, home, sweet, sweet, home!
dear - er than all. Home, home, sweet, sweet, home!

There's no place like home, There's no place like home.

156   Soldiers' Chorus.

G. F. R.

Risoluto.

Arranged.

1. Not a tear, not a fear, At the bu-gle's sounding; Haste a-way—
2. Hear the drum ! see them come ! Shall we fal-ter? nev-er! Wrong must fail,

no de-lay, Soldiers, brave and true; Sa-bers clash—helmets flash,
right pre-vail— Raise our ban-ners high. Hear the shout ring-ing out,

Cres.   m   Fine.

Ev-ery heart is bound-ing; Comes the call, "Forward all !" Home and friends, adieu.
Lib-er-ty for-ev-er! Firm-ly stand, sword in hand, We will do or die.

f   m

Forward now, on our captain's word re-ly-ing, Forward now, all our
Forward now, on our captain's word re-ly-ing, Forward now, all our

Cres.

country's foes de-fy-ing; Loud-ly now, hear the bat-tle-cry re-
country's foes de-fy-ing; Loud-ly now, hear the bat-tle-cry re-

sound, Yes, loud hear the bat-tle-cry, the bat-tle-cry re-sound.

Never Forget the Dear Ones.

G. F. ROOT.

Andantino.

1. Nev - er for - get the dear ones A - round the so - cial hearth,
2. Ev - er their hearts are turn - ing To thee when far a - way,
3. Nev - er for - get thy fa - ther, Who cheerful toils for thee,

The sun - ny smiles of glad - ness, The songs of art - less mirth
Their love so pure and ten - der, Is with thee on thy way.
With - in thy heart may ev - er Thy moth - er's im - age be;

Tho' oth - er scenes may woo thee In oth - er lands to roam,
Wher-ev - er thou may'st wan - der, Wherev - er thou may'st roam,
Thy sis - ter and thy broth - er, They long for thee to come,

Nev - er for-get the dear ones That clus - ter round thy home.

Oh, the Rain!

Children may sing freely from the Base staff (boys especially.) The pitch will be an octave higher than base voices sing, but that is of no consequence here.

GEO. F. ROOT.

Moderato.

1. Oh, the pleas-ant sum - mer rain, We are glad to hear a - gain,
2. Oh, the pleas -ant sum - mer rain, Life and health the drops con -tain,

With its beau - ti - ful re - frain, On the roof and the tree:
That from off my win - dow pane To the grass gen - tly fall:

And we know the wel-come sound Brings a joy to all a - round,
They re-fresh the sul - try air, They make ev-'ry flow'r more fair;

On the dry and thirst - y ground, Far as eye can see.
And a beau - ty, fresh and rare, They im - part to all.

REFRAIN.

Hear the pat-ter, pat-ter, pat-ter, pat-ter, pat-ter, pat-ter, pat-ter, pat-ter,

Hear the rain, drop - ping, drop - ping

pleasant summer rain, Yes, the pat - ter, pat - ter, pat - ter, pat - ter,

down, Pleasant summer rain,

pat - ter, pat - ter, pat - ter, pat - ter, beau - ti - ful re - frain; Dropping,

drop - ping, drop - ping, beau - ti - ful re - frain; Dropping

pat - ter, pat - ter, pat - ter, pat - ter, pat - ter, pat - ter, pat - ter, pat - ter

down, drop - ping, drop - ping

on the thirsty ground, Speaking, pat - ter, pat - ter, pat - ter, pat - ter,

down on the thirsty ground,

pat - ter, pat - ter, pat - ter, pat - ter, joy for all a - round. . . . .

Giv - ing joy to all a - round, to all a - round.

List! 'tis Music Stealing.

This may be sung as a Duet, or by singing from Base staff, as a Trio.

Moderato.

Arranged.

1. List! 'tis mu - sic steal-ing O - ver the rip - pling sea;
2. Mu - sic sounds the sweet-est, When o'er the rip - pling sea
3. List! a - gain 'tis steal-ing O - ver the rip - pling sea;

Key of B flat.

Bright you moon is beam-ing O - ver each tow'r and tree; The
Our bark sails,—the fleet-est,—To a sweet mel-o - dy; Then
Min - gling with our num-bers, Like fair - y har - mo - ny; Then

Key of E flat.

waves seem list'ning to the sound As si - lent - ly they flow, O'er
as we glide o'er waters clear We'll sing that plaintive strain, Which
sail and sing far o'er the wave, In moonlight's sil - ver glow, O'er

cor - al groves and fair-y ground, And sparkling caves be-low.
mem'ry makes to each so dear, And home re-calls a - gain.
cor - al groves and fair-y ground, And sparkling caves be-low.

"I Ought," "I Will."

Geo. W. Bungay.

G. F. R.

Maestoso.

1. There are two gi - ants in the land, Of stalwart strength and
2. "I ought," to hon - or is a - kin, And con-science is its
3. "I will," a war-rior stout and brave, Was nev - er yet pol-
4. How they have helped the world a - long With force-ful speech and

stature grand; What tasks of du - ty they ful - fill When-ev - er
light with-in; It sees what du - ties to ful - fill, If "baf fled
troon or slave—With justice armed, it conquers still, Up - on the
ring-ing song, In commerce, cul-ture, sci-ence, skill; And tow'ring

they join heart and hand! One is "I ought,"and one "I will." "I
oft," is sure to win, When aided by the pow'r "I will." "I
land, and on the wave; Hail just "I ought," and brave "I will." "I
still a - mid the throng, Are firm "I ought," and bold "I will." "I

ought," "I ought," One is "I ought," and one "I will."
"I will," "I will," When aid ed by the pow'r "I will."
ought," "I ought," Hail just "I ought,"and brave "I will."
"I will," "I will," Are firm "I ought." and bold "I will."

Maestoso.

1. March, and let your heart be glad! In your
2. Let not sor-row dim your eye; Soon shall
3. On-ward then to bat-tle move; More than

Christian sol-dier,

heav'nly ar-mor clad; Fight! nor think the bat-tle
ev-'ry tear be dry; Let not fear your course im-
conqu'ror you shall prove; Tho' op-posed by many a

Christian sol-dier,

long; Vic-t'ry soon will crown your song.
pede; Great your strength if great your need.
foe, Chris-tian sol-dier, on-ward go.

Christian sol-dier,

CHORUS.

March! march! march! Let your heart be strong,

March, and let your heart be strong, March, and let your heart be strong,

Vic-t'ry soon will crown, will crown your song.

Vic-t'ry soon will crown your song, will crown, will crown your song.

(D. S. "To the sign.") JEFFREY.

Allegretto.

1. The sum - mer days are com - ing, The blos-soms deck the bough;
D. S. reign is near - ly o - ver, The spring is on the wane,
2. The min - strel of the moon-light, The love - lorn night - in - gale,
D. S. sum - mer days are com - ing, The blos-soms deck the bough
3. We'll rise and hail thee ear - ly, Be - fore the sun hath dried
D. S. sum - mer days are com - ing, The blos-soms deck the bough,

Fine.

The bees are gai - ly humming, And the birds are sing-ing now;
Oh, haste thee, gen - tle sum - mer, To our pleas-ant land a - gain!
Has sung his month of mu - sic To the rose-queen of the vale;
The bees are gai - ly humming, And the birds are sing-ing now!
The dew-drops that will spar - kle On the green hedge by our side;
The bees are gai - ly humming, And the birds are sing-ing now!

We have had our May-day garlands, We have crown'd our May-day queen,
And what tho' he be si - lent, As the night comes slow-ly on!
And when the blaze of noon-day Glares up - on the thirst - y flow'rs,

D. S.

With a cor - o - net of ros - es, Set in leaves of brightest green. But her
We'll have dances on the greensward, To sweet mu - sic of our own! Oh, the
We will seek the welcome cov - ert Of our jasmine shaded bow'rs! Oh, the

Stars Trembling O'er Us.

The third part is here written upon the Treble staff. Sing without instrument, when well learned.

MISS MULOCH. GEO F. ROOT.

1. Stars trembling o'er us, And sun-set be-fore us, Mountains in
2. Come not, pale sor-row, De-part till to-mor-row; Rest soft-ly
3. Waves soft-ly cov-er The depths we glide o-ver, So let the
4. Heaven clear above us, Bless all who love us, All whom we

sha-dow, And for-ests a-sleep.
fall-ing, O'er eye-lids that weep. While down the riv-er We
past in For-get-ful-ness sleep.
love in Thy ten-der-ness keep.

float on for-ev-er, Speak not, oh, breathe not, There's peace on the deep.

Softly Sighs the Breeze.

G. F. R.

1. Soft-ly sighs the summer breeze,   Thro' the green and leafy
2. Birds of song their voices lend,   With the sighing breeze to
3. All a-round is bright and fair,   Earth is clothed in beauty

sum-mer breeze,
voic-es lend,
bright and fair,

trees; .... Warbling mu - sic soft and low, ...
blend; ... Bright-hued flow-ers, sweet and gay, ...
rare, ... Flow -ers bloom and breez - es play, ...

leaf - y trees;   soft and low,
breeze to blend;   sweet and gay,
beau - ty rare,   breez -es play,

As the murm'ring brooklet's flow. .....
Smile a - long our lone - ly way. .....
On this love - ly ver - nal day. .....

the murm'ring brooklet's flow.
a - long our lone - ly way.
this love - ly ver - nal day.

If I Were A Sunbeam.

m Andantino.   *f*   ✱

1. If I were a sun - beam, I know what I would do,
2. Steal-ing in a - mong them, The brightest light I'd shed,
3. And while all looked up - ward, I there would shine and shine,

dim.   *m*

I'd go in - to the hov - els, All dark with want and woe.
Un - til each wea - ry suf - f'rer With new hope raised his head.
Un - til they thought of heav - en, Their own sweet home and mine.

The Hammer Song.

G. F. R.   G. F. R.

It would be a good plan for the girls to sing the duet, and the boys, in two divisions, the "kling, klang."

Allegretto.

1. To the din of the an - vil's ring - ing,
2. To the fire of the forg - es glanc - ing,

Klang, klang, klang, klang, klang, klang klang,

Kling, kling, kling, kling, kling, kling, kling, kling,

And the voice of the sharp steel sing - ing, Join the song, mer - ry
And the stars of the i - ron danc - ing, Join the song, mer - ry

klang, klang, klang, klang, klang, klang, klang,

kling, kling, kling, kling, kling, kling,

song, Of the hammer blows so clear and strong. Join the song,

klang, klang, klang, klang, klang, klang, klang,

kling, kling, kling, kling, kling, kling, kling, kling,

mer-ry song, Of the ham-mer blows so clear and strong.

klang, klang, klang, klang, klang, klang, klang.

kling, kling, kling, kling, kling, kling, kling.

The Whirlwind.

JAMES HUNGERFORD.

G. F. R.

1. The whirlwind! the whirlwind! a mon-arch is he;
2. The soft winds that nour-ish the blos-soms and flow'rs
3. He comes on his char-iot—the grand, loft-y cloud;

And he sways a wide re-gion—the land and the sea,
Flee a-way from the for-est, the fields, and the bow'rs;
And the voice of his com-ing is haughty and loud;

And who is so daunt-less that bends not in fear When he
To cav-erns of still-ness in ter-ror they hie, For they
He vaunt-eth his strength, and he shouts in his glee, That no

pass-es a long in his might-y ca-reer?
know that the king of the tem-pest is nigh,
spir-it of storm is so might-y as he,

When he pass-es a-long in his might-y ca-reer.
For they know that the king of the tem-pest is nigh.
That no spir-it of storm is so might-y as he.

The Roses.

QUARTET FOR LADIES' VOICES.

G. F. Root.

1. The ro - ses, the ro - ses, Are blush-ing bright and gay;
2. The ro - ses, the ro - ses, How bright their soft leaves shine;

The lil - y bells are bend - ing low Be - neath the sun - god's ray;
While star-eyed daisies peep be - neath The dain - ty eg - lan - tine;

The pan - sies spread their vel - vet leaves Beneath the smil - ing skies,
The blackbird whis - tles on the bough With notes of joy - ous mirth,

And dew - drops lie like tears with - in The vio - let's meek blue eyes,
And count-less flow -ers sweet-ly bloom To deck the joy - ous earth,

And dew-drops lie like tears within The vio - let's meek blue eyes.
And countless flow - ers sweetly bloom To deck the joy - ous earth.

If convenient let Tenors and Basses join in Chorus to give all parts.

LIZZIE A. BINKERD.   W. H. CLARKE.

DUET.

1. A band of scholars, now we come, The parting hour draws near;
2. There let us nev - er cease to learn, But wis-dom seek and find;
3. Oft will we wish, in years to come, We could live o'er a - gain
4. And now, although life's journey lies In paths ne'er trod be - fore,

To bid good-bye to teachers kind, To friends and classmates dear.
Our school will be the wide, wide world, Our teach-ers, all man-kind.
Those joys which youth alone can know, A - las! such wish were vain.
May we all meet at God's high throne, To dwell there ev - er - more.

CHORUS.

To dear school days, a long farewell! Now dawns another life;

May each one no - bly act his part, And conquer in the strife.

The Brook-Miller's Song.

G. F. R.

G. F. Root.

Boys, or low Alto voices, sing from Base staff. When well learned, sing in three parts without accompaniment.

Moderato.

1. I work, I sing, my mill is al-ways go-ing,
For down the hill the brook is al-ways flow-ing,
2. For miles a-round the boys their grain are bringing,
And that you see keeps mill and me a sing-ing,

1. I work, I sing,
For down the hill,
2. For miles a-round,
And that you see,

From morn till night, thro' all the sum-mer day;
And while it runs, my wheel can nev-er stay;
And glad they give the toll I take for pay;
From morn till night, thro' all the sum-mer day;

From morn till night,
And while it runs
And glad they give
From morn till night

Oh, glad and free the song my mill-wheel sings me,

Oh, glad and free

While loud the brook goes laugh-ing on its way, And

while loud

that is why my mill is al-ways go-ing, go-ing, go-ing, go-ing,

go-ing, go-ing, go-ing, go-ing all the sum-mer day.

Hurrah for the Country.

I. WALTON.

Con anima.

1. Hurrah for the coun-try, the joy-ous, the free! Hurrah, boys, hurrah!
2. Exchange thou the gas-lights for beauti-ful stars! Hurrah, boys, hurrah!
3. Hurrah for the coun-try, pure air and blue sky! Hurrah, boys, hurrah!
4. Hurrah for the land that blooms freely for all! Hurrah, boys, hurrah!

Where wild breezes dal-ly with each leaf-y tree, Hurrah, boys, hurrah!
And moonbeams that send down their silver-y bars, Hurrah, boys, hurrah!
Hur-rah for the breez-es that mer-ri-ly fly, Hurrah, boys hurrah!
For bird-notes of mu-sic and trout brooklet's fall, Hurrah, boys, hurrah!

Queen of the Silent Night.

New Arrangement.

1st Soprano.

1. Hail to thee, queen of the si - lent night, Shine clear, shine bright

2d Soprano.

2. Dart thy pure beams from thy throne on high, Beam on thro' sky

Alto.

yield thy pen-sive light; Blithely we'll dance in thy sil - ver ray,

robed in a - zure dye; We'll laugh and sport while the night-bird sings,

Hap-pi - ly pass - ing the hours a - way; Yes, yes, we love the

Flapping the dew from her sa - ble wings, Sprites love to sport in

stil - ly night, Dressed in her robes of blue and white; Heav'n's arches ring,

still moonlight, Sprinkling the pear s of shad'wy night; Then let us sing,

Queen of the Silent Night. Concluded. 173

Stars wink and sing, Hail, si - lent night! Fair - y moon-light,

Time's on the wing, Hail, si - lent night! Fair - y moon-light,

fair - y moon-light, Fair - y, fair - y, fair - y moon-light.

fair - y moon-light, Fair - y, fair - y, fair - y moon-light.

Fair - y moon - - - - - light.

How Many Miles?

Gently.

1. How ma - ny miles to Ba - by Land? A - ny one can tell:
2. What do they do in Ba - by Land? Dream, and wake, and play;
3. What do they do in Ba - by Land? Why, the odd - est things;
4. Who is the queen in Ba - by Land? Moth-er, kind and sweet;

Up one flight, To the right; Please to ring the bell.
Laugh and crow, Shout and grow; Jol - ly time have they.
Might as well Try to tell What a bir - die sings.
And her love, Born a - bove, Guides the lit - tle feet.

The Colony, or Far Away to Idaho.

After this piece has been learned by all, select voices to take the different characters.

M. B. C. SLADE.   G. F. R.

Boy with knapsack and staff.

1. I'm bound to raise a col - o - ny, to start for I - da - ho;

In all this pleas-ant com - pa - ny, oh, who would like to go?

Soldiers.

You need an es - cort, bold and brave, to guard you on the way;

We sol - dier boys our guns will have, and start this ver - y day.

CHORUS. (*Girls and all.*)

Hur-rah, hurrah, then, who will go, Far a - way to I - da - ho? Hur-

The Colony, or Far Away to Idaho. Concluded. 175

rah, hur-rah, then, who will go, Far a-way to I - da - ho?

Lumbermen, Carpenters, Farmers, Millers.

2 We'll take the ax, we *Lumbermen*, and hew the timber down;
  We *Carpenters* will saw it then, and build a splendid town;
  We *Farmer-boys* will sow the plain, and reap the golden field;
  We *Millers* all will grind your grain, the meal and flour to yield.—*Cho.*

Smiths.

3 Your picks and bars will soon be broke; our anvils we will bring,
  And blow on blow the merry stroke shall from the smithy ring.

Shoemakers.

  The Rocky Mountains tramping o'er, your shoes will be worn out,
  We shoemakers will make you more, and sew them strong and stout.—*Cho.*

Post-Master and Merchant.

4 I'll keep the Post-office for you, and send your letters well;
  And *I* will keep in my new store all kinds of things to sell.

Builders.

  We'll build a church and school-house there, for those things we must have;
  And just beneath the cross, on high, the stars and stripes shall wave!—*Cho.*

The whole company.

5 Now let us clasp the friendly hand and promise, one and all,
  To keep a true, unbroken band, whatever may befall;
  So give a cheer, brave company, for Idaho, the fair,
  And for the splendid Colony we're bound to carry there!—*Cho.*

The Shepherd's Song.

J. R. MURRAY.   Arranged.

1. Down from the loft-y mountains, Where all the day we shepherds roam;
2. Cheer-ful our song is ring-ing, Nev-er a fear or care we know;
3. Now from all care and sor-row We come with lightsome hearts and gay;
4. For sim-ple joys are last-ing, And sim-ple pleas-ures safe and true;

Has-ten we to the fount-ains, And pleas-ant vales of home.
Hear how the hills our sing-ing Re-ech-oes as we go.
Hop-ing to taste to-mor-row, What we en-joy to-day.
No shad-ow o-ver-cast-ing, To make us sigh for new.

Far Away the Camp Fires Burn.

Beautiful effect with boys or Alto voices singing the third part from base staff. When well learned, sing without instrument.

MERCADANTE.

Allegretto.

1. Far a - way the camp fires burn; We can see their rud - dy light
2. Onward, brothers, for the right, Blessings on you, as you go;

From the dist - ant hill-tops flash, Bright'ning up the brow of night.
Pan -o - plied for freedom's fight, Nought but blessing shall we know.

There our brave boys watch and wait, While at home, both night and day,
From our al - tars prayers a - rise, From our homes shall songs ascend,

Ad lib.

Mem'ries sweet we treasure up Of the ab - sent far a - way:
He who rul - eth in the skies, Shall your ev'ry step de - fend:

Tempo.

There our brave boys watch and wait, While at home, both night and day,
From our al - tars prayers a - rise, From our homes shall songs ascend;

Mem-'ries sweet we treas-ure up   Of the ab-sent far a - way.
He who rul - eth in   the skies, Shall your ev'ry step de - fend.

Thus while they a - far   for free-dom fight, Our spir-its yet   shall

ev - er yearn For that hap - py day, when they shall all   vic-

to - ri - ous   re - turn.   Oh, hast - en, hap - py day!   Oh,

hast - en, hap-py day! Oh, hast-en, hast -en, hap-py   day!

The Passing Seasons. (A Cantatina.)

M. B. C. SLADE.

GEO. F. ROOT.

Select eighteen children to personate and sing the first 18 verses, as follows.—Old Year, 1st verse; New Year, 2d verse; Spring, 3d; March, 4th; April, 5th; May, 6th; Summer, 7th; June, 8th; July, 9th; August, 10th; Autumn, 11th; September, 12th; October, 13th; November, 14th; Winter, 15th; December, 16th; January, 17th; February, 18th. All sing 19th and 20th verses, and also the part marked "Chorus," which comes after 6th, 10th, 14th, 18th, and 20th verses.

As a school exercise this may be sung by having the 18 children, in turn, rise in their places, and sing their verses, the school remaining seated until the 19th verse, then all rise to end with. To give it more elaborately, all but the 18 could be seated back on a stage, (or, as the piece is not very long, they could stand, if there is not room for seats.

There should be a raised seat for a throne in the center, with "Old Year" in it at the beginning,—the other 17 being out of sight. But they come on, one by one, promptly, in their turn, so that as quick as one is through, the next begins.

Old Year, New Year, and Winter should be boys, but the other 15 should be girls. Old Year hands his scepter to New Year as he leaves the throne. New Year remains on the throne during the piece. Old Year should pass out of sight after leaving the throne, but may return to the chorus after divesting himself of his aged appearance (if he is in costume).

After each solo, (which should be sung well in front,) let the singer pass to such a position that at the end, Spring and Summer and their months will be on one side of the throne, and Autumn and Winter with their months on the other. They may be a little in front of throne, and two deep, if there is not room for a single line.

The stage may be decorated with evergreens and flowers, but the piece is so short that it would not be worth the while to do much in this way. So with costumes. Flowers, Grasses, Wreaths, (green, or autumn leaves, according to season,) Holly berries, Baskets of fruits, etc., may be used by the singers according to their part, on their dresses, or in their hands.

Old Year might have a long gray garment, a long white beard, and a faded crown. New Year brighter garments, and a new crown. Winter could have a dark garment, with cotton wool for snow flakes, and alum crystals for frost. He wears a low crown, while Spring, Summer, and Autumn wear wreaths. The solo singers join in chorus after they get upon the stage.

1. Ah, well! ah, well! I sad-ly tell, My mo-ments fleet are fly-ing!
2. I come! I come! I haste a-long, The throne, the scep-ter tak-ing!

Like dis-tant chime of Christmas bell, The Old Year's hours are dy-ing!
Ap-pear, oh, loy-al subject throng, Your choice of serv-ice mak-ing.

Good-night! good-night! good-by! good-by! My long bright reign is end-ing;
Come Au-tumn, Win-ter, Summer, Spring, With wondrous va-ried grac-es;

I   see glad New Year drawing nigh, My   hap - py throne as-cend-ing.
And 'round the sun the earth we'll bring, A - long the   star - ry   spa-ces.

Allegretto.

3. The Spring! the joy - ous Spring am I! My handmaids see   me bringing!
7. A - way, bright Spring! my maids I bring, And each a   wel-come com-er;
11. Sweet Summer, haste! for on   I   fly To hang my gold-en treasure
15. My crown of ice,   my robe of snow, My frost - y   san-dals wearing,

Ca - pri - cious A - pril, will - ful March, And May with mu-sic ring-ing.
The brook shall laugh, the val - leys sing, To greet the sun - ny sum-mer.
On branch-es low, and branch-es high, Bright Autumn's fullest meas-ure.
Be - fore my brave young troop I go, An i - cy scep-ter bear-ing.

4. The driving storm, the rush-ing gale, Be-cause you need, I send you,
8. With daisies deck'd, with ros - es crown'd, I bring the wild bees' humming,
12. I crowd with fruits the tree, the vine, And glad young hearts re-mem-ber,
16. See gay De - cem - ber drawing near! Glad Christmas I am bring-ing,

But clear blue gleams, o'er hill and vale, Thro' rift - ed clouds I lend you.
And cal-low nest-lings chirp around, When gen-tle June is com-ing.
The Autumn leaves that glow and shine O'er joy - ous, gay Sep-tem-ber.
With Christmas gift, and song and cheer, And mer - ry bells a - ring-ing.

Giojoso.

5. You find the grass, the buds, the leaves, Where thro' the show'r I fling them,
9. Be - fore me, glowing bright Ju - ly, Flies ev - ery cloud and shad-ow,
13. And I in for - ests, gay no more, From woodlands brown and so-ber,
17. With sleigh bells chime and coast-ers' glee, And skat-ers' shout, so mer - ry,
Chorus.
19. Re - joice! re-joice! in tune - ful song, Raise all our hap - py voic-es,

And swallows build be-neath the eaves, When home a-gain I bring them.
While brilliant flow'rs of deep - est dye, I spread o'er hill and mead-ow.
Shake down of nuts the children's store, In frost - y, keen Oc - to - ber.
Glad New Year smiles to wel-come me, His own bright Jan - u - a - ry.
The Months and Sea-sons haste a - long, And ev - ery heart re - joic - es.

6. And I, yes, I'm the mer-ry May! The ap-ple trees are blooming,
10. And I dance o'er the sun-ny plain, A wealth of har-vest find-ing,
14. I wear no ros-es on my brow, But Au-tumn leaf-lets growing,
18. Last come I, changeful month that stands 'Twixt Winter's bind-ing pow-ers,
20. Re-joice! re-joice! a-gain re-joice! He reigns in beau-ty o'er us,

And rob-in-redbreast's round-e-lay, Sings out, to greet my com-ing.
Where mer-ry reap-ers reap the grain That mer-ry maids are binding.
And chill No-vem-ber, soft and low, Sings, "Autumn time is go-ing."
And Spring, bright maid, whose tender hands Set free the buds and flow-ers.
We greet the New Year on his throne, With full re-sound-ing cho-rus.

CHORUS, by all who are on the stage, gradually including the whole school.

We come! we come! Each sea-son brings her du-ty; We'll
A-way! a-way! With all our gen-tle pow-ers We
We come! we come! At sun-set hear them sing-ing, While
'Tis o'er! 'tis o'er! The har-vest mer-ry mak-ing, And
He reigns! he reigns! He reigns in beau-ty o'er us! We

crown the love-ly earth our home, With joy and light and beau-ty.
break a-way the ice and snow, And strew the earth with flow-ers.
o'er the new-mown fields they roam, And "Harvest-home" is ring-ing.
to the gold-en Au-tumn days. Our leave we now are tak-ing.
greet the New Year on his throne, With full re-sound-ing cho-rus.

182 Cold Water for Me.

Arranged.   Arranged.

1. Cold wa-ter, cold wa-ter for me, There's nothing so pure and so
2. There's nothing like wa-ter to give The strength that we need while we
3. Nor am I a-lone in my choice; There's ma-ny a mu-si-cal

free, I'll go to the brook, and I'll go to the
live; And so to the stream, or the brook, or the
voice Will join at the stream, or the brook, or the

spring, And o-ver its bub-bles I'll shout and I'll sing.
spring, I'll haste and I'll drink, and I'll mer-ri-ly sing.
spring, And o-ver their bub-bles we'll mer-ri-ly sing.

Cold wa-ter, cold wa-ter, cold wa-ter, cold wa-ter for me.

Cold wa-ter, cold wa-ter, cold wa-ter, cold wa-ter for me.

Moderato.

1. Walk! walk! walk! A doub-le-quick gal-lop or trot, Yes, walk! walk! walk!
2. Look! look! look! Your eyes growing heavy and red; And stare! stare! stare!
3. Where next, where? And what is re-main-ing to see? My heart grows faint,
4. Drag! drag! drag! All jad-ed and wea-ry, a-long, And watch! watch! watch

So wea-ry, and gasping, and hot; All down thro' one long endless aisle;
To beat the things in-to your head! It nev-er, no nev-er would do
With toils that are wait-ing for me; At Nor-way I start on my tour,
Oh, this is the Main Building song. In eight-y days, once on a time,

Then up thro' an-oth-er, no stop— Oh, this is the way the Main
To come to this won-der-world fair, And when you get home be un-
Thro' It-a-ly next I must go, And Denmark, and Sweden, and
The whole world was seen—so they say—But we have complete-ly put

Build-ing is seen, Un-til you are read-y to drop.
a-ble to tell The won-der-ful things you saw there.
Rus-sia, and Spain, All swell the dread list of my woe!
that in the shade, By see-ing it all in one day.

Beautiful Evening Star.

1. Star of the eve - ning, glad - ly we hail thee, Now, as thou
2. Bright beacon - light of wan - der - ers wea - ry, Shin - ing a -
3. Star of the eve - ning, now as thou beam - est Soft ly up -

shin - est down from a - far, Now, when the shades of twi - light are
bove them wher-e'er they roam, Guide thou the way-worn trav - el - er's
on us, down from a - far, Sweet is thy smile, se - rene in thy

deep - 'ning, Beau - ti - ful, beau - ti - ful eve - ning star.
foot - steps Safe to the wait - ing ones dear at home.
glo - ry, Beau - ti - ful, beau - ti - ful eve - ning star.

p CHORUS.

Beau-ti - ful star! beau - ti - ful star! Star of the

Beau - ti - ful star! Beau-ti - ful star!

Cres.

eve - ning, beau - ti - ful star! Beauti - ful star!

Cres.

Star of the eve - ning, beau-ti - ful star! Beau - ti - ful star!

beau - ti - ful star!   Star of the evening, beau-ti - ful star!

beau - ti - ful star!

The Holiday.

G. F. R.   Arranged.

Moderato.

1. 'T is just the time for free - dom, Just the time for fun,
2. 'T is just the time to ride in, Just the time to row,
3. Oh, yes, it pays to work well Ev - 'ry day and hour,

And we can take them hon - est - ly, For all our work is done;
'T is just the time for an - y-thing, That's fair and right to do;
It pays to keep an hon - est heart, And break the temp-ter's pow'r.

We 've learn'd and said our les - sons, We 've put our books a - way,
So bring the ball and bat, boys, And ev - 'ry kind of play,
For when the work is done, boys, Oh, who so free and gay,

Hur - rah for fun and frol - ic, boys, It is our hol - i - day.
And let's be off to-geth - er, for It is our hol - i - day.
As they who 've earn'd the right to have A glo-rious hol - i - day.

The Workers. (Boys.)

First Division. From "Silver Lute."

1. I am a lit - tle *farm - er,* My pro - duce is all cheap;
2. I am a lit - tle *blacksmith,* I'll set your hors - es shoe;
3. I am a lit - tle *hat - ter,* Your head I'll cov - er well;

Chorus. We all are mer - ry *Work - ers,* We'll keep in pleas - ant mood;

Second Division.

And I'm a lit - tle *mil - ler,* The nic - est flour I keep;
And I'm a lit - tle *carpen - ter,* I'll make a house for you;
And I'm a lit - tle *tin - ner,* My wares I wish to sell;

No mat - ter what our *trade* is, If we're but do - ing good;

Third Division.

And I'm a lit - tle *bak - er,* As neat as e'er was seen;
And I'm a lit - tle *tai - lor,* I war - rant all my suits;
And I'm a lit - tle *paint - er,* Don't let your house get gray;

The world is wide and need - y, And if we all are true,

Fourth Division.

And I'm a lit - tle *butch - er,* My shop is bright and clean.
A *shoe - mak - er* am I, sir,—Pray, buy a pair of boots.
And I'm a lit - tle *den - tist,* Don't let your teeth de - cay.

The world will be the bet - ter For what we *Work - ers* do.

The Workers. (Girls.)

First Division.
1 I make up ladies' *dresses,*
In fashionable style;

Second Division.
The ladies' *caps* and *bonnets*
I'm trimming all the while;

Third Division.
And I keep knitting *stockings,*
For gents and ladies too;

Fourth Division.
And I the yarn am *spinning—*
I work as hard as you.

First Division.
2 I 'tend the *loom* and *shuttle*,
  To make the cloth you wear;

Second Division.
  I make sweet yellow *butter*,
  And *cheese* that's rich and rare;

Third Division.
  In making pretty *straw-braid*,
  I make my fingers fly;

Fourth Division.
  I sell nice *tapes* and *muslins*
  To all who choose to buy.

First Division.
3 I *teach* the little children
  To read, and write, and spell;

Second Division.
  The sick I go a *nursing*,
  To help them all get well;

Third Division.
  I visit all the *poor* folks,
  And give them bread to eat;

Fourth Division.
  And I my *house* keep *keeping*,
  A housewife trim and neat.
Chorus. We all are merry, etc.

NOTE. While singing the Chorus to the first "WORKERS," let each work according to his trade. Thus: 1, the farmer sows; 2, the miller grinds; 3, the baker kneads; 4, the butcher cuts. Again: 1, the blacksmith strikes; 2, the carpenter saws; 3, the tailor sews; 4, the shoemaker sews. Again: 1, the hatter brushes; 2, the tinner hammers; 3, the painter brushes; 4, the dentist files.

In the second "WORKERS," the Chorus is exactly the same. The dress makers sew; the milliners arrange ribbons; the knitters knit; and the spinners whirl the spinning wheel with the right hand. The weavers throw the shuttle from right to left; the dairy folks churn; the braiders braid; and the shop-keepers measure with a yard-stick.

What Say the Birds?

Swing the Bright Hammer.

Allegro.

1. Swing the bright ham-mer, boys, Swing for the blow, Strike the hot
2. Hark! how the woodlands ring, Hark! for each blow, Strike while they

1. Swing! swing! Swing for the blow, Strike!
2. Hark! hark! Hark! for each blow, Strike!

i - ron, boys, By the red glow; See the bright spark-lets fly,
an - swer, boys, By the red glow; Now while the shad-ows fall,

strike! By the red glow; See! see!
strike! By the red glow; Now! now!

Hiss - ing they go, Strike the hot i - ron, boys, By the red glow.
Som - ber and slow, Strike the hot i - ron, boys, By the red glow.

Hiss - ing they go, Strike! strike! By the red glow.
Som - ber and slow, Strike! strike! By the red glow.

There is a modulation here to the key of G. It would be well to apply the syllables accordingly through the entire section.

Hear the old an - vil ring, Mer - ri - ly, oh! Sing out the
Hear the clear ech - oes wake, Sweet-ly they flow, Sing out the

Hear the old an - vil ring, Mer - ri - ly, oh! Sing out the
Hear the clear ech - oes wake, Sweet-ly they flow, Sing out the

Swing the Bright Hammer. Concluded. 189

Key of C.

cho - rus, boys, Sing for each blow; Swing the bright ham-mer, boys,

cho - rus, boys, Sing for each blow; Swing! swing!

Swing for the blow, Strike the hot i - ron, boys, By the red glow.

Swing for the blow, Strike! strike! By the red glow.

Morning.

J. R. MURRAY.   G. F. R.

Allegretto.

1. O'er the hill-top streaming, ... Lakes and riv-ers gleaming,
2. Now be-fore it flee - ing, ... Hills and valleys waking,
3. O - ver land and o - cean, ... Earth in glad commotion,

See the morning's light;
Sweep the shades of night;
Floods its gold-en streams;

In its beams so bright. Awake! Awake! Rejoice in morning's light.
Greet the glowing light. Awake! Awake! Rejoice in morning's light.
Welcomes morning's beams. Awake! Awake! Rejoice in morning's beams.

A - wake! A - wake! Awake!

Oh, Yield Thee not to Sorrow.

The upper part may be sung by a single voice, or by a few voices.

TYROLEAN.

1. Oh, yield thee not to sor - row, Tho' clouds are in the
2. The cheer - ful, gold - en sun - shine Will fall up - on thy

1. Oh, yield thee not to sor - row, Tho' clouds are in the
2. The cheer - ful, gold - en sun - shine Will fall up - on thy

sky, la, la, la, la, la, la, la, la,
heart, la, la, la, la, la, la, la, la,

sky la, la, la, la, la, la, la, la, la, la, la, la, la, la,
heart, la, la, la, la, la, la, la, la, la, la, la, la, la, la,

la, la, la, la, la, la, la, la, la, la,

la, la, la, la, la, la, la, la, la, la, la, la, la, la, la,

la, They'll van - ish on the mor - row, When south-winds waft them
la, And joy will beam more bright-ly As shades of night de-

la, la, la, They'll vanish on the mor - row, When south-winds waft them
la, la, la, And joy will beam more bright-ly As shades of night de-

by, They'll van-ish on the mor-row When south winds waft them by.
part, And joy will beam more brightly As shades of night de-part.

by, They'll van-ish on the mor-row, When south winds waft them by.
part, And joy will beam more brightly As shades of night de-part.

Beautiful Things.

The melody of this piece is in the Third Part. †††
Andantino.

1. There are beau - ti - ful things in this world of ours For those who will
2. And the bird-choirs u - nite in the an-them grand, And bright waters
3. Oh, how hap - py are they that shall rest be - side Those streams that are

live in the light; Its breez - es, and sunshine, and ver - nal show'rs, Its
chant on the sea; And streamlets go murmur-ing thro' the land At-
liv - ing and clear; And watch the bright waters that soft - ly glide 'Mid

mountains of snow and its vales of flow'rs, Its day and its deep'ning night.
tuned by the won-der-ful Mas-ter-hand, As parts in the har - mo - ny.
pas - tures of par - a-dise, green and wide, With nevermore care nor fear.

Give Welcome to the Swallow.

F. KUCKEN. New arrangement.

DUET.

1. Give wel-come to the swal - low, He news of summer brings; A-
2. Ye lit - tle play-ful lamb-kins, Ye here can safe - ly stay, Ye
3. Fare-well, then, to the swal - low, He skims a - long the plain, The

cross the sea, a - far comes he With sun-shine on his wings. But
fear no harm, with fleece so warm, From win-ter's bit - ter day. But
home he leaves beneath the eaves He soon will seek a - gain. But

when the leaves are fall - ing, No lon - ger will he stay, But
when the leaves are fall - ing, And bar - ren is the spray, But
fast the leaves are fall - ing, He can not lin - ger here, But

when the leaves are fall - ing, No lon - ger will he
when the leaves are fall - ing, And bar - ren is the
fast the leaves are fall - ing, He can not lin - ger

stay. He hur-ries past from winter's
spray, The swallow flies to brighter
here. When sweet birds sing, in ear - ly

He hur-ries past, from winter's blast,
The swal-low flies to brighter skies,
When sweet birds sing, in ear-ly spring,

blast, Far, far a - way, far,
skies, Far, far a - way, far,
spring, He will ap - pear, he

He hur-ries past, from win-ter's blast, He hur-ries
Far, far a - way the swallow flies, To brighter
He will ap - pear when sweet birds sing, In ear - ly

far . . . . . a - way,   He flies a-
far . . . . . a - way,   He flies a-
will . . . . . ap - pear,   When sweet birds

past, From winter's blast he flies a - way, Far, far a - way,
skies, The swallow flies to brighter skies, Far, far a - way,
spring, He will appear, he will ap - pear, When sweet birds sing,

way,   Far, far a - way,   far,
way,   Far, far a - way,   far,
sing,   He will ap - pear,   he

From winter's blast,   He hur - ries past from win - ter's
The swal-low flies,   The swallow flies to brighter
He will ap - pear,   In ear-ly spring, when sweet birds

far . . . . . a - way,   From   win-ter's
far . . . . . a - way,   To   brighter
will . . . . . ap - pear,   When   sweet birds

blast, He hur-ries past, Far, far a - way,   From   win-ter's
skies, He flies a - way, Far, far a - way,   To   bright-er
sing, He will ap-pear, He will ap - pear,   When   sweet birds

blast He hur-ries past, Far, far a - way. . . . .
skies He flies a - way, Far, far a - way, ...
sing, He will ap -pear, He will ap - pear. . . . .

A Song for May. *

Allegretto.

1. A song, a song for beauti -ful May, Floating o - ver the hills to-day,
2. A song, a song for beauti -ful May, Floating o - ver the hills to-day,
3. A song, a song for beauti -ful May, Floating o - ver the hills to-day,
4. Then welcome, welcome, beautiful May, Floating o - ver the hills to-day,

With scarf of mist and robe of light, Wov-en of sunbeams fair and bright.
With dain-ty vi - 'let-slippered feet, Tripping thro' valleys low and sweet.
A deep-er blue is in the sky, Soft -er the breeze goes whisp'ring by.
With scarf of mist and voice of song, Singing her carols the whole day long.

A song, A song,

A song for May, A song for May.

Parting Song.

J. R. MURRAY.

From New C. & C., by per.

1. One more song, and then we sev-er; One more clasp of hands, and then

2. Sweet the mem'ries that shall lin-ger Round this dear fa - mil - iar place;

We must part, per-haps for - ev - er, Tho' we'll hope to meet a - gain.

Mem-o - ries of song and sing-er, Tho'ts which time can not ef - face.

Life's great school is now be - fore us, Tho' our training here may end;

Faithful friends and dear com-panions, All we've known and loved so well,

May the same kind love be o'er us, Where-so - e'er our ways may tend.

Now has come the hour of parting, Now we bid you all fare-well.

HYMNS.

Devotion. 11s.

HYMN 1.

GEO. F. ROOT.

1. We praise thee—we bless thee, our Fa - ther and Friend,
2. We thank thee for bless - ings re - ceived ev - 'ry day—
3. Pro - tect us— de - fend us from sin and from harm,

Oh, let our de - vo - tions be - fore thee as - cend;
For which thou hast taught us un - ceas - ing to pray;
As the shep - herd doth gath - er the lambs with his arm;

In youth and in child - hood to - geth - er we come,
But oh, for the treas - ures thy word hath in store,
Oh, nour - ish and strength - en our souls now in youth,

To pray that thy will in our hearts may be done.
Thy name, oh, our Fa - ther, we bless and a - dore.
With thy love and thy wis - dom— thy good - ness and truth.

(197)

Hillsdale. L. M.

HYMN 2. BLACKLOCK.

GEO. F. ROOT.

1. Come, O my soul! in sa-cred lays, Attempt thy great Cre-a - tor's praise;
2. Enthroned amid the radiant spheres, He glo-ry like a gar - ment wears;

But oh, what tongue can speak his fame, What mortal voice can reach the theme.
To form a robe of light di-vine, Ten thousand suns a-round him shine.

3 In all our Maker's grand designs,
Almighty power, with wisdom shines;
His works, thro' all this wondrous frame,
Declare the glory of his name.

4 Raised on devotion's lofty wing,
Do thou, my soul, his glory sing;
And let his praise employ thy tongue
Till list'ning worlds shall join the song!

HYMN 3.   KEN.

1 Awake, my soul, and with the sun
Thy daily stage of duty run;
Shake off dull sloth, and joyful rise,
To pay thy morning sacrifice.

2 Glory to thee, who safe hast kept,
And hast refreshed me while I slept;
Grant, Lord, when I from death shall wake,
I may of endless life partake.

3 Lord, I my vows to thee renew;
Scatter my sins as morning dew;
Guard my first springs of thought and will,
And with thyself my spirit fill.

4 Direct, control, suggest, this day,
All I design, or do, or say;
That all my powers, with all their might,
In thy sole glory may unite.

HYMN 4.   WATTS.

1 With all my powers of heart and tongue,
I'll praise my Maker in my song;
Angels shall bear the notes I raise,
Approve the song, and join the praise.

2 Amid a thousand snares, I stand
Upheld and guarded by thy hand;
Thy words my fainting soul revive,
And keep my dying faith alive.

3 I'll sing thy truth and mercy, Lord;
I'll sing the wonders of thy word;
Not all thy works and names below
So much thy power and glory show.

HYMN 5.   WATTS.

1 Bless, O my soul, the living God;
Call home thy thoughts that rove abroad;
Let all the powers within me join
In work and worship so divine.

2 Bless, O my soul, the God of grace;
His favors claim the highest praise;
Why should the wonders he hath wrought
Be lost in silence and forgot?

3 Let every land his power confess;
Let all the earth adore his grace;
My heart and tongue with rapture join,
In work and worship so divine.

HYMN 6.   WATTS.

1 From all that dwell below the skies,
Let the Creator's praise arise:
Let the Redeemer's name be sung,
Thro' ev'ry land—by ev'ry tongue.

2 Eternal are thy mercies, Lord;
Eternal truth attends thy word;
Thy praise shall sound from shore to shore,
Till suns shall rise and set no more.

HYMN 7. WATTS.   From " New C. and C.," by per.

1. Give thanks to God; he reigns above; Kind are his thoughts, his name is love:
2. He feeds and clothes us all the way, He guides our footsteps lest we stray;
3. Oh, let our hearts with joy record The truth and goodness of the Lord!

His mer-cy a -ges past have known, And a - ges long to come shall own.
He guards us with a pow'r-ful hand, And brings us to the heav'nly land.
How great his works! how kind his ways! Let every tongue pronounce his praise

HYMN 8.   WATTS.

1 Give to our God immortal praise;
Mercy and truth are all his ways;
Wonders of grace to God belong;
Repeat his mercies in your song.

2 Give to the Lord of lords renown,
The King of kings with glory crown:
His mercies ever shall endure,
When lords and kings are known no more.

3 He built the earth, he spread the sky,
And fixed the starry lights on high:
Wonders of grace to God belong:
Repeat his mercies in your song.

4 He fills the sun with morning light,
He bids the moon direct the night:
His mercies ever shall endure,
When suns and moons shall shine no more.

HYMN 9.   PALGRAVE.

1 Lord God of morning and of night,
We thank thee for thy gift of light:
As in the dawn the shadows fly,
We seem to find thee now more nigh.

2 O Lord of light, 'tis thou alone
Canst make our darkened hearts thine
own;
Though this new day with joy we see,
O dawn of God, we cry for thee.

3 Praise God, our Maker and our Friend;
Praise him through time, till time shall end;
Till psalm and song his name adore
Through Heaven's great day of Evermore.

HYMN 10.   NEEDHAM.

1 Awake, my tongue, thy tribute bring
To him who gave thee power to sing:
Praise him, who is all praise above,
The source of wisdom and of love.

2 Through each bright world above, behold
Ten thousand thousand charms unfold;
Earth, air, and mighty seas combine,
To speak his wisdom all divine.

HYMN 11.   CONDER.

1 The Lord is King! lift up thy voice,
O earth, and all ye heavens, rejoice!
From world to world the joy shall ring,
The Lord omnipotent is King!

2 The Lord is King! who then shall dare
Resist his will, distrust his care?
Holy and true are all his ways:
Let every creature speak his praise.

HYMN 12.   ANON.

1 Lord God of hosts, by all adored!
Thy name we praise with one accord;
The earth and heavens are full of thee,
Thy light, thy love, thy majesty.

2 Loud hallelujahs to thy name
Angels and seraphim proclaim;
Eternal praise to thee is given
By all the powers and thrones in heaven.

3 From day to day, O Lord, do we
Highly exalt and honor thee;
Thy name we worship and adore,
World without end, forevermore.

Rosehill. L. M.

HYMN 13. WATTS.

J. E. SWEETSER.

1. Awake, our souls! a - way, our fears! Let ev-ery trembling thought be gone;
2. True, 'tis a strait and thorny road, And mortal spir-its tire and faint;

A-wake, and run the heavenly race, And put a cheer - ful cour-age on!
But they for - get the might-y God, Who feeds the strength of ever-y saint.

3 The mighty God, whose matchless power
Is ever new and ever young,
And firm endures, while endless years
Their everlasting circles run.

4 From thee, the overflowing spring,
Our souls shall drink a fresh supply;
While such as trust their native strength
Shall melt away, and droop, and die.

Rockingham. L. M.

HYMN 14. TATE and BRADY.

DR. MASON.

1. Oh, ren-der thanks to God a-bove, The fountain of e - ter - nal love;
2. Who can his might-y deeds ex-press, Not on - ly vast—but number-less?

Whose mer-cy firm, thro' a - ges past, Hath stood, and shall forev - er last.
What mor - tal el - oquence can raise His trib-ute to im-mor-tal praise?

3 Extend to me that favor, Lord,
Thou to thy chosen dost afford;
When thou return'st to set them free,
Let thy salvation visit me.

4 Oh, render thanks to God above,
The fountain of eternal love:
His mercy firm, through ages past,
Hath stood, and shall forever last.

Rosedale. L. M.

HYMN 1b. WATTS.

GEO. F. ROOT.

1. Lord, thou hast searched and seen me through; Thine eye commands, with piercing view,
2. My thoughts, before they are my own, Are to the Lord dis-tinct-ly known;

My rising and my resting hours, My in-most heart, and all my powers.
He knows the words I mean to speak, Ere from my open-ing lips they break.

3 Within thy circling power I stand;
On every side I find thy hand;
Awake, asleep, at home, abroad,
Still present with me is my God.

4 Oh, may these tho'ts possess my breast,
Where'er I rove, where'er I rest!
Nor let my weaker passions dare
Consent to sin, for God is there.

Federal St. L. M.

HYMN 16. WATTS.

H. K. OLIVER.

1. God of the morn-ing, at thy voice The cheerful sun makes haste to rise,
2. Oh, like the sun may I ful-fill The appointed duties of the day;

And like a gi-ant doth re-joice To run his journey thro' the skies.
With ready mind, and ac-tive will, March on, and keep my heavenly way.

3 Lord, thy commands are clean and pure,
Enlightening our beclouded eyes;
Thy judgments just, thy promise sure;
Thy gospel makes the simple wise.

4 Give me thy counsels for my guide,
And then receive me to thy bliss;
All my desires and hopes beside
Are faint and cold compared with this

Dedham. C. M.

GARDINER.

1. Once more, my soul, the ris - ing day Sa-lutes thy wak -ing eyes;
2. Night unto night his name re-peats, The day re - news the sound,
3. Great God, let all my hours be thine, While I en - joy the light;

Once more, my voice, thy trib - ute pay To him that rules the skies.
Wide as the heaven on which he sits, To turn the sea-sons round.
Then shall my sun in smiles de - cline, And bring a pleasant night.

HYMN 18. WARDLAW.

1 Lift up to God the voice of praise,
 Whose breath our souls inspired;
Loud, and more loud, the anthems raise,
 With grateful ardor fired.

2 Lift up to God the voice of praise,
 Whose goodness, passing thought,
Loads every moment as it flies,
 With benefits unsought.

3 Lift up to God the voice of praise,
 For hope's transporting ray,
Which lights through darkest age of death,
 To realms of endless day.

HYMN 19. WATTS.

1 Oh, that the Lord would guide my ways,
 To keep his statutes still!
Oh, that my God would grant me grace,
 To know and do his will!

2 Oh, send thy spirit down, to write
 Thy law upon my heart;
Nor let my tongue indulge deceit,
 Nor act the liar's part.

3 Order my footsteps by thy word,
 And make my heart sincere;
Let sin have no dominion, Lord,
 But keep my conscience clear.

4 Make me to walk in thy commands,
 'Tis a delightful road;
Nor let my head, nor heart, nor hands,
 Offend against my God.

HYMN 20. WATTS.

1 Eternal Wisdom! thee we praise,
 Thee the creation sings;
With thy loved name rocks, hills and seas,
 And heaven's high palace rings.

2 Thy hand, how wide it spreads the sky,
 How glorious to behold!
Tinged with a blue of heavenly dye,
 And starr'd with sparkling gold.

3 Infinite strength and equal skill
 Shine through thy works abroad;
Our souls with vast amazement fill,
 And speak the builder, God!

HYMN 21. WATTS

1 O thou, to whom all creatures bow
 Within this earthly frame;
Through all the world, how great art t' os !
 How glorious is thy name!

2 When heaven, thy beauteous work on high,
 Employs my wandering sight;
The moon that nightly rules the s y,
 With stars of feebler light;—

3 Lord, what is man, that thou sho' 1st deign
 To bear him in thy mind!
Or what is race, that thou should t prove
 To them so wondrous kind!

4 O thou, to whom all creatures bow,
 Within this earthly frame,
Through all the world, how great art thou !
 How glorious is thy name!

HYMN 22. ANON.   DR. MASON.

1. God of my life, my morn-ing song To thee I cheer-ful raise;
2. Preserved by thy al-mighty arm, I passed the shades of night,

Thine acts of love 'tis good to sing, And pleasant 'tis to praise.
Se-rene, and safe from ev-'ry harm, To see the morn-ing light.

3 Oh, let the same almighty care
  Through all this day attend;
From every danger, every snare,
  My heedless steps defend.

4 Smile on my minutes as they roll,
  And guide my future days;
And let thy goodness fill my soul,
  With gratitude and praise.

HYMN 23.   DODDRIDGE.

1 Awake, my soul, stretch every nerve,
  And press with vigor on;
A heavenly race demands thy zeal,
  And an immortal crown.

2 A cloud of witnesses around
  Hold thee in full survey;
Forget the steps already trod,
  And onward urge thy way.

3 'Tis God's all-animating voice,
  That calls thee from on high;
'Tis his own hand presents the prize
  To thine aspiring eye.

HYMN 24.   WATTS.

1 Lord, in the morning thou shalt hear
  My voice ascending high;
To thee will I direct my prayer,
  To thee lift up mine eye.

2 Thou art a God before whose sight
  The wicked shall not stand;
Sinners shall ne'er be thy delight,
  Nor dwell at thy right hand.

HYMN 25.   WESLEY.

1 Blest be the everlasting Lord,
  Our Father, God and King!
Thy sov'reign goodness we record,
  Thy glorious power we sing.

2 By thee the victory is given;
  The majesty divine,
Wisdom and might, and earth and heaven,
  And all therein, are thine.

3 The kingdom, Lord, is thine alone,
  Who dost thy right maintain,
And, high on thy eternal throne,
  O'er men and angels reign.

4 Thou hast on us the grace bestowed,
  Thy greatness to proclaim;
And, therefore, now we thank our God,
  And praise his glorious name.

HYMN 26.   ANON.

1 Great God, in whom we live and move,
  Accept our feeble praise,
For all the mercy, grace, and love,
  Which crown our youthful days.

2 For countless mercies, love unknown,
  Lord, what can we impart?
Thou didst require one gift alone,
  The offering of the heart.

3 Incline us, Lord, to give it thee;
  Preserve us by thy grace,
Till death shall bring us all to see
  Thy glory face to face.

Stephens. C. M.

HYMN 27. LOGAN.

WM. JONES.

1. Oh, hap-py is the one who hears In - struc-tion's warning voice;
2. For she hath treasures great-er far Than east and west un - fold;

And who ce - les -tial wis - dom makes His ear - ly, on - ly choice.
And her re-wards more precious are Than all their stores of gold.

3 She guides the young with innocence
  In pleasure's path to tread;
  A crown of glory she bestows
  Upon the hoary head.

4 According as her labors rise,
  So her rewards increase;
  Her ways are ways of pleasantness,
  And all her paths are peace.

Evan. C. M.

HYMN 28. THOMSON.

Arr. by DR. MASON.

1. Je - ho - vah God! thy gracious power On ev - ery hand we see;
2. Thy power is in the o - cean deeps And reaches to the skies;
3. In all the vary - ing scenes of time, On thee our hopes de - pend;

Oh, may the bless - ings of each hour Lead all our thoughts to thee.
Thine eye of mer - cy nev - er sleeps, Thy goodness nev - er dies.
In ev - ery age, in ev - ery clime, Our Fa - ther and our Friend.

Olmutz. S. M.

HYMN 29. WATTS.   ARr. by DR. MASON.

1. Thy name, Al - might - y Lord, Shall sound thro' dis - tant lands;
2. Far be thine hon - or spread, And long thy praise en - dure,

Great is thy grace, and sure thy word, Thy truth for - ev - er stands.
Till morning light, and evening shade, Shall be exchanged no more.

Laban. S. M.

HYMN 30.   DR. MASON.

1. My soul, be on thy guard, Ten thousand foes a - rise;
2. Oh, watch, and fight, and pray! The bat - tle ne'er give o'er;

The hosts of sin are press - ing hard To draw thee from the skies.
Re - new it bold-ly ev - ery day, And help di - vine im-plore.

3 Ne'er think the victory won,
  Nor once at ease sit down;
Thy arduous work will not be done
Till thou obtain thy crown.

4 Fight on, my soul, till death
  Shall bring thee to thy God!
He'll take thee at thy parting breath
Up to his blest abode.

Nuremburg 7s.

HYMN 31. BARBAULD.

AHLE.

1. Praise to God, im-mor-tal praise, For the love that crowns our days;
2. For the bless-ings of the field, For the stores the gar-dens yield,

Boun-teous Source of ev-ery joy, Let thy praise our tongues em-ploy.
For the joy which harvests bring, Grateful prais-es now we sing.

3 All that Spring, with bounteous hand,
Scatters o'er the smiling land ;
All that liberal Autumn pours
From her rich o'erflowing stores.

4 Lord, for these our souls shall raise
Grateful vows and solemn praise;
And when every blessing's flown,
Love thee for thyself alone.

Pleyel's Hymn. 7s.

HYMN 32. ANON.

J. PLEYEL.

1. Heav'nly Fa-ther, sov'reign Lord, Be thy glo-rious name a-dored!
2. Though unworth-y, Lord, thine ear, Deign our hum-ble songs to hear;
3. While on earth or-dained we stay, Guide our footsteps in thy way,

Lord, thy mer-cies nev-er fail; Hail, ce-les-tial good-ness, hail!
Pur-er praise we hope to bring, When a-round thy throne we sing.
Till we come to dwell with thee, Till we all thy glo-ry see.

HYMN 33.   FAWCETT.   ARR. by Dr. MASON.

1. Praise to thee, thou great Cre-a-tor! Praise to thee from every tongue:
2. Fath-er, Source of all compassion, Pure, un-bound-ed grace is thine:

Join, my soul, with ev-ery crea-ture, Join the u-ni-ver-sal song.
Hail the God of our sal-va-tion! Praise him for his love di-vine.

3 For ten thousand blessings given,
    For the hope of future joy,
Sound his praise through earth and heaven,
    Sound Jehovah's praise on high.

4 Joyfully on earth adore him,
    Till in heaven our song we raise;
There, enraptured, fall before him,
    Lost in wonder, love, and praise.

HYMN 34.   ROBINSON.

1 Mighty God! while angels bless thee,
    May a mortal lisp thy name?
Lord of men, as well as angels!
    Thou art every creature's theme:

2 Lord of every land and nation!
    Ancient of eternal days!
Sounded through the wide creation,
    Be thy just and glorious praise.

3 For the grandeur of thy nature,—
    Grand, beyond a seraph's thought;
For the wonders of creation,
    Works with skill and kindness wrought;

4 For thy providence, that governs
    Through thine empire's wide domain,
Wings an angel, guides a sparrow;
    Blessed be thy gentle reign.

HYMN 35.   MANT.

1 Praise the Lord! ye heavens, adore him,
    Praise him, angels in the height;
Sun and moon, rejoice before him;
    Praise him, all ye stars of light!

2 Praise the Lord—for he hath spoken;
    Worlds his mighty voice obeyed,
Laws which never shall be broken,
    For their guidance he hath made.

3 Praise the Lord—for he is glorious;
    Never shall his promise fail;
God hath made his saints victorious,
    Sin and death shall not prevail.

4 Praise the God of our salvation,
    Hosts on high his power proclaim:
Heaven and earth, and all creation,
    Laud and magnify his name.

HYMN 36.   ONDERDONK.

1 Blest be thou, O God of Israel,
    Thou, our Father, and our Lord!
Blest thy majesty forever!
    Ever be thy name adored.

2 Thine, O Lord, are power and greatness,
    Glory, victory, are thine own;
All is thine in earth and heaven,
    Over all thy boundless throne.

3 Riches come of thee, and honor,
    Power and might to thee belong;
Thine it is to make us prosper,
    Only thine to make us strong.

4 Lord, to thee, thou God of mercy,
    Hymns of gratitude we raise;
To thy name, forever glorious,
    Ever we address our praise!

Sicilian Hymn. 8s & 7s.

HYMN 37. BOWRING. SICILIAN AIR.

1. God is love; his mer-cy brightens All the paths in which we rove;
2. Ev'n the hour that dark-est seem-eth Will his changeless goodness prove;
3. He with earth-ly cares en-twineth Hope and comfort from a-bove:

Bliss he wakes, and woe he lightens; God is wisdom, God is love.
From the gloom his brightness streameth; God is wisdom, God is love.
Ev-'ry-where his glo-ry shin-eth; God is wisdom, God is love.

Vesper Hymn. 8s & 7s.

HYMN 38. OSLER. OLD MELODY.

1. Wor-ship, hon-or, glo-ry, blessing, Lord, we of-fer to thy name; }
   Young and old, their thanks express-ing, Join thy goodness to pro-claim: }
2. As the hosts of heav'n adore thee, We, too, bow, be-fore thy throne; }
   As the an-gels serve before thee, So on earth thy will be done. }

Ju-bi-la-te, Ju-bi-la-te, Ju-bi-la-te. A-men.

Italian Hymn. 6s & 4s.

HYMN 39. ANON.   GIARDINI.

1. God of the morn-ing ray, God of the ris-ing day,
2. God of our fee-ble race, God of re-deem-ing grace,

Glo-rious in power! In thee we live and move, And thus we
Spir-it all-blest! Our own e-ter-nal Friend, Thy guar-dian

dai-ly prove Thy con-de-scend-ing love Each pass-ing hour.
in-fluence lend, From ev-'ry snare de-fend, In thee we rest.

Arlington. C. M.

HYMN 40. ANON.   Dr. ARNE.

1. E-ter-nal source of life and light, Su-premely good and wise,
2. Our dark and err-ing minds illume With truth's celes-tial rays;
3. Safe-ly con-duct us by thy truth, Thro' life's perplex-ing road;

To thee we bring our grate-ful vows; Ac-cept our sac-ri-fice.
In-spire our hearts with heav'nly love, And tune our lips to praise.
And bring us, when our jour-ney's o'er, Lord, to thine own a-bode.

Spanish Hymn. 6s & 5s.

HYMN 41. ANON.

Spanish.

1. Thro' thy pro-tect-ing care, Kept till the dawn - ing, Taught to draw
2. God of our sleeping hours, Watch o'er us wak - ing, All our im-

near in pray'r, Heed we the warn - ing; Now from night's bondage free,
per-fect pow'rs, In thine hands tak - ing; In us thy work ful - fill,

Glad-ly our souls would be, Worthily praising thee, God of the morn-ing.
Be with thy chil-dren still, Those who obey thy will, Nev - er for - sak - ing.

Badea. S. M.

HYMN 42. WATTS.

German.

1. Come—sound his praise a - broad, And hymns of glo - ry sing;
2. Come—wor-ship at his throne, Come—bow be - fore the Lord;

Je - ho - vah is the sov-ereign God, The u - ni - vers - al King.
We are his work, and not our own, He formed us by his word.

HYMN 43. A. L. WARING.

1. In heav'n-ly love a-bid-ing, No change my heart shall fear,
2. Wherev-er he may guide me, No want shall turn me back;
3. Green pastures are be-fore me, Which yet I have not seen;

And safe is such con-fid - ing, For noth-ing chang-es here;
My Shep-herd is be-side me, And noth-ing can I lack!
Bright skies will soon be o'er me, Where darkest clouds have been.

The storm may roar with-out me, My heart may low be laid,
His wis-dom ev-er wak-eth, His sight is nev-er dim,
My hope I can not meas-ure, My path to life is free;

But God is round a-bout me, And can I be dis-mayed?
He knows the way he tak-eth, And I will walk with him.
My Sav-ior has my treas-ure, And he will walk with me.

HYMN 44. HAWEIS.

1 To thee, my God and Savior!
  My heart exulting sings,
Rejoicing in thy favor,
  Almighty King of kings!
I'll celebrate thy glory,
  With all thy saints above,
And tell the joyful story
  Of thy redeeming love.

2 Soon as the morn, with roses
  Bedecks the dewy east,
And when the sun reposes
  Upon the ocean's breast,
My voice, in supplication,
  Well-pleased the Lord shall hear:
Oh! grant me thy salvation,
  And to my soul draw near.

HYMN 45. MONTGOMERY.

1 God is my strong salvation,
  What foe have I to fear?
In darkness and temptation,
  My Light, my Help is near;
Though hosts encamp around me,
  Firm in the fight I stand;
What terror can confound me,
  With God at my right hand?

2 Place on the Lord reliance;
  My soul, with courage wait;
His truth be thine affiance,
  When faint and desolate:
His might thy heart shall strengthen,
  His love thy joy increase;
Mercy thy day shall lengthen;
  The Lord will give thee peace!

America. 6s & 4s.

HYMN 46. ANON.　　　　　　　　　　　　　　Old Melody.

1. God bless our na - tive land, May heav'n's pro-tect-ing hand
2. May just and right - eous laws Up - hold the pub - lic cause,
3. And not this land a - lone, But be thy mer - cies known

Still guard our shore. May peace her power ex - tend, Foe be trans-
And bless our name; Home of the brave and free, Stronghold of
From shore to shore; Lord, make the na - tions see That men should

formed to friend, And all our rights de-pend On war no more.
Lib - er - ty, We pray that still on thee There be no stain.
broth - ers be, And form one fam - i - ly, The wide world o'er.

HYMN 47.　　　　　　S. F. SMITH.

1 My country, 'tis of thee,
Sweet land of liberty,
　Of thee I sing;
Land where my fathers died,
Land of the pilgrim's pride,
From ev'ry mountain side
　Let freedom ring.

2 My native country! thee,
Land of the noble free,
　Thy name I love;
I love thy rocks and rills,
Thy woods and templed hills;
My heart with rapture thrills,
　Like that above.

3 Let music swell the breeze,
And ring from all the trees
　Sweet Freedom's song;
Let mortal tongues awake,
Let all that breath partake;
Let rocks their silence break,
　The sound prolong.

HYMN 48.　　　　Tune: Pleyel's Hymn, p. 206.

1 Suppliant, lo, thy children bend,
　Father, for thy blessing now;
Thou canst teach us, guide, defend,
　We are weak, Almighty thou!

2 With the peace thy word imparts
　Be the taught and teacher bless'd;
In our lives and in our hearts,
　Father, be thy laws impress'd.

Our Father in Heaven.

HYMN 49. ANON.

Portuguese Air.

1. Our Fa - ther in heav - en, we hal - low thy name,
2. For - give our trans - gres - sions, and teach us to know

May thy king-dom ho - ly on earth be the same;
That hum - ble com - pas - sion that par - dons each foe;

Oh, give to us dai - ly our por - tion of bread, ..
Keep us from temp - ta - tion, from weak - ness, and sin, ...

For 'tis from thy boun - ty that all must be fed, ..
And thine be the glo - ry, and thine be the glo - ry,

For 'tis from thy boun - ty that all must be fed.
And thine be the glo - ry, for - ev - er. A men.

INDEX.

(214)

216   Index.

www.ingramcontent.com/pod-product-compliance
Lightning Source LLC
Chambersburg PA
CBHW030819270326
41928CB00007B/808